TRAINS
1921–1939

ADAM JOŃCA

POLISH ARMOURED TRAINS 1921–1939

VOL. 3

Published in Poland by
STRATUS s.j., ul. Żeromskiego 6A
27-600 Sandomierz, Poland
e-mail: office@mmpbooks.biz
as MMPBooks
e-mail:rogerw@mmpbooks.biz
© 2023 MMPBooks
http://www.mmpbooks.biz
Copyright © 2023 Adam Jońca
Copyright © 2023 Stratus s.j.

ISBN
978-83-67227-37-7

Editor in Chief: Roger Wallsgrove
Editorial Team: Bartłomiej Belcarz, Artur Juszczak, Robert Pęczkowski
Author: Adam Jońca
Cover: Dariusz Wyżga
Layout Design: Bartłomiej Belcarz
Translation: Artur Przęczek
Proof-reading: Konrad Przeczek

Printed by
Wydawnictwo Diecezjalne
i Drukarnia w Sanodmierzu
www.wds.pl

PRINTED IN POLAND

Photographs: the author's collection, Tomasz Basarabowicz, Bogusław Bobel, [the late] Pascal Danjou, Jacek Haber, Artur Przęczek, Sławomir Kordaczuk, Dariusz Kowalczyk, Krzysztof Kuryłowicz, [the late] Janusz Magnuski, Paul Malmassari, Krzysztof Margasiński, Wawrzyniec Markowski, Mariusz Zimny, *Centralne Archiwum Wojskowe (Wojskowe Biuro Historyczne)* – Central Military Archives (Military Historical Bureau), *Archiwum Dokumentacji Mechanicznej (Narodowe Archiwum Cyfrowe)* – Archives of Mechanical Documentation (National Digital Archives), *Ośrodek "Karta"* – The "Karta" Centre, *Muzeum Wojska Polskiego* – Polish Army Museum, *Muzeum Historyczne w Legionowie* – Historical Museum in Legionowo, *Muzeum Niepołomickie* – Museum of Niepołomice.

Colour profiles: by the author – based on technical reconstruction drawings by Artur Przęczek, [the late] Witold Jeleń, [the late] Leszek Komuda and the author.

Special thanks to Mr. Artur Przęczek for creating and providing reconstructions of technical drawings of rolling stock, coaches, wagons and steam locomotives.

Translator's notes: the abbreviation P.P. – *pociąg pancerny* (armoured train) is applied throughout the book. The names of the individual armoured trains are retained in Polish. The abbreviation *wz.00 – wzór"* (issue / model) distinctively identifies any given piece of military equipment by the year of introduction.

INTRODUCTION

Armoured trains were extremely crucial weapon systems in the Polish-Ukrainian War of 1918–1919 and the Polish-Bolshevik War of 1919–1920. The dominating feature of both wars was manoeuvrability – hardly ever the battle-lines were truly defined. In mobile warfare with unstable fronts, combat trains were a formidable and effective weapon.

The exact number of armoured trains created in the period 1918–1921 cannot be established. There were several dozen of them – some operated for a very short time. The names, numbers and assignments changed, as well as the rolling stock composition. Some trains were assembled from whatever materials and armaments were at hand, and were described as armoured trains in a somewhat optimistic manner. Sometimes they did not even appear on the official weapon registries.

Depending on what criteria is applied, in total there were 85, maybe even 90 Polish combat trains. Those days and those trains require a special study – it is being prepared and will be released in the not too distant future. It will be the volume **"Polish Armoured Trains 1918–1921"**, in the same format and with the same narrative method as in this publication.

This volume begins in 1921 – after the war with Soviet Russia – and ends in September 1939 – the German invasion, followed 17 days later by the treacherous Soviet attack, thus starting a new Great War, this time designated as number "Two".

In a separate study, we plan to present armoured trains, undoubtedly Polish, but not belonging to the Polish Army. Such are the Polish trains of the I Corps formed in Russia in 1917, so when the Independent Republic of Poland had not yet existed, and the trains from Arkhangelsk and Novorossiysk, allied to the Entente, and formally belonging to the Polish Army in France, a separate Polish armed force combined with the Polish Army in the country only in September 1919.

„Polish-non-Polish" were also trains of the Central Lithuania army existing as a separate state from October 1920, after the so-called rebellion of *Generał* Lucjan Żeligowski, joined to the Polish in April 1922. The Army of Central Lithuania was an autonomous formation, under its own command.

The situation of Polish trains in the Wielkopolska Uprising was similar, although for different reasons. The Autonomous Greater Poland Army began to merge with the Polish Army in December 1919. Before that time, and after the victory of the uprising, the Greater Poland Army was operationally subordinate to the orders of the Polish Army, but inside it governed itself.

In Silesia, during the Third Uprising, the insurgent army was subordinate to the Supreme Command of the Insurgent Forces and only after the victory the Silesian armored trains formally became trains of the Polish Army, and the temporary I. Upper Silesian Armoured Train Regiment was disbanded only in 1923.

In September 1939, 10 regular armoured trains went into battle; a few improvised trains were created during the September Campaign.

To those who unwisely claim that armoured trains were wasted money and misused equipment assets, since even a single enemy aircraft could easily disable this obsolete weapon system... it is worth remembering, that these mobile four-gun artillery batteries – that is what in fact the armoured trains were – managed to inflict considerable losses to the enemy. It is also worth to emphasize that the P.P. 54 *"Groźny"* – the train with the shortest combat history – was not eliminated by the enemy, but only by a bridge that was prematurely blown up by retreating Polish troops. Armoured trains P.P. 53

"Śmiały", P.P. 55 *"Bartosz Głowacki"* and P.P. 51 *"Marszałek"* were in full working order after three weeks of defensive fighting. Armoured train P.P. 52 *"Piłsudczyk"* also remained in operation for three weeks and was intentionally derailed by the crew when the ammunition supply was exhausted. In the course of the campaign, in a single encounter, P.P. 53 *"Śmiały"* was able to demolish a large number of the German *Panzer Division* tanks during the battle of Mokra.

While it is true that anti-aircraft defences of the Polish armoured trains were inadequate, an addition of the modern "Bofors" 40 mm anti-aircraft gun allowed for a success in fending off enemy aerial assaults. Both, P.P. 51 *"Marszałek"* and P.P. 55 *"Bartosz Głowacki"* were supplemented by such guns during the campaign.

During the course of the 1939 defensive war, there was an enormous effort on part of the armoured train crews to dissolve huge railroad traffic jams. Many track repairs were very efficiently carried out – the training paid off.

So let us do justice to the heroic actions of the crews and pay tribute to the armoured trains of the Polish Army...

TABLE OF CONTENTS

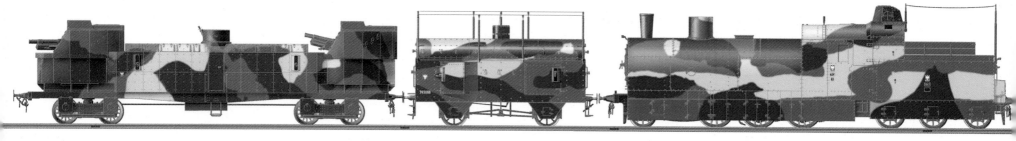

ARMOURED TRAINS 1930–1939
2. DYWIZJON POCIĄGÓW PANCERNYCH (2nd ARMOURED TRAIN GROUP)

2. Dywizjon Pociągów Pancernych (*2nd Armoured Train Group*). *A commemorative field mass on the occasion of Group's holiday in 1933 or 1934.*

2nd ARMOURED TRAIN GROUP

On 8 April 1928 the 1st Regiment of Railway Pioneers (*Pułk Saperów Kolejowych*) stationed at Niepołomice organized the 2nd Armoured Train Group (*Dywizjon Pociągów Pancernych*). After decommissioning of P.P. 8 "Stefan Czarniecki" (and at the same time, P.P. 12 "Zagończyk" in 1st Armoured Train Group) a new roster was composed, and in 1930 the combat configuration of the 2nd Group was as follows:

Armoured Train No. 5 "Śmiały"
- artillery wagon 699020,
- artillery wagon 699021,
- assault wagon 627950,
- armoured draisines.

Armoured Train No. 6 "Groźny"
- artillery wagon 450012,
- artillery wagon 460025,
- assault wagon 631550,
- armoured draisines.

Armoured Train No. 7 "Piłsudczyk"
- artillery wagon 699069,
- artillery wagon 699070,
- assault wagon 402633,
- armoured draisines.

Armoured Train No. 9 "I. Marszałek"
- artillery wagon 460022,
- artillery wagon 460023,
- assault wagon 393088 (ex – 140866),
- armoured draisines.

Armoured Train No. 10 "Bartosz Głowacki"
- artillery wagon 630728 (ex-02005),
- artillery wagon 630729 (ex-02029,

Civilian and enlisted technicians of the 2. Dywizjon workshop, Niepołomice, October of 1934.

- assault wagon 630726,
- armoured draisines.

Armoured Exercise Train of the Reserve Detachment (*Pociąg Pancerny Szkolny Dywizjonu Zapasowego*)
- to be assembled from reserve combat equipment.

The bulk of the armoured equipment was stationed at the Bonarka railroad sidings. The "I. Marszałek" was designated as an operational cadre train, while the rest of the equipment was considered a mobilization reserve. Troop barracks – one story buildings – were also located at the Bonarka depot. The equipment was warehoused at the provisional buildings located at the Płaszów station.

The exchange of the rolling stock between the Armoured Groups was overseen by the unit commanders, pending approval of their respective Railway Regiments. The process was completed without any significant issues. In the middle of 1930's the replacements were compete, the com-

D.O.K.Nr.V. - 2.dyon poc.panc.

ZESTAWIENIE

mat.uzbr.,potrzebnego na wyposażenie mob.pociągów pancernych wg.etatów Organizacji poc.panc.na stopie wojen.L.100/Org.Tjn.30.
Oddziału I.Szt.Głównego.

Nazwa pociągu pancern.	Części składowe poc.panc.	Jednostka mob.	3" ap.nb.ros.wz.02.	10 cm. as.wz.14.	CKM. nm. fs. wz. 08.	CKM. nm. wz. 25.	LKM. nm. 08/ 15.	Kbk. wz. 98.	Pi-stolu-ty.sw.	Pi-sto-le-ty.	Heł-my.	Pa-sy do kbk.ce rm.pop.trój-ne	ża-ki do wni-kle-ety do kb wz.98.	Żab-naty 3"ap.ros.10cm. wz. 98.	Gra-nele ap.rs. cm.hb.wz.02.	Szrap-naty do 3" hb.as. wz.14.	Gra-nele 10cm. as.wz.14.	Szrap- do KM 7,92 m/m.	Nb. do kb. wz. 98.	Rakiety osw.sygn.	Granaty ręczne zacz.obr.	Nb. do pisto-le-tow	UWAGI:
Nr.5. "Śmia- ły"	Dca poc.panc. z poczt.i druż.adm.	2 dyon p.p.						27	8	-	4	-	27	54	35				-	2160	120	80	48	24	-	1/ Nb.do kbk.ustalono wg.normy: po 120 nb.dla szereg.plut.szturmowego i po 80 nb.dla szereg.pozostałych części pociągu pancernego.
	Plut.ogniowe I/5 i II/5.	- " -	4	10				46	2	-	-	-	46	92	48	po 300 nb.na działo pol.i po 200 nb.na hb.pol.	300000	3680	-	-	192	96	-	
	Plut.szturmowy	20.p.p.				2		25	3	-	29	25	50	28		60000	3000	-	-	112	56	-	2/ Granaty ręczne ustalono: a/dla 12 szer.sekcji łączn.po 6 gr. = 72.
	" techniczny	1.baon most.kol.						14	1	-	-	14	28	15		-	1120	-	-	-	-	-	b/ " 2.of.i 46 szer./bez ordyn./ I.i II plut.ogniowych = 48 x 6 gr.= 288
	Drezyna pancerna	2.dyon p.p.				2		-	5	-	-	-	-	-		60000	-	-	-	20	100		c/dla 1.of.i 27 szer./bez ordyn./ plut.szturmowego = 28 x 6 gr. = 168
Nr.6. "Groźny"	Dca poc.panc. z poczt.i druż.adm.	2 dyon p.p.						27	8	-	4	-	27	54	35		-	2160	120	80	48	24	-	d/dla 5 szereg.drezyny panc.x 6 gr. = 30
	Plut.ogniowe I/6. i II/6.	- " -	4	10				46	2	-	-	-	46	92	48	jak wyżej	300000	3680	-	-	192	96	-	Razem: 558 gr.ręcz
	Plut.szturmowy	20.p.p.				2		25	3	-	29	25	50	28		60000	3000	-	-	112	56	-	
	" techniczny	1.baon most.kol.						14	1	-	-	14	28	15		-	1120	-	-	-	-	-	3/ Odnośna poprawka do tabel mob.,zmieniająca jedn.mobilizującą plutonu szturmowego poc.panc.Nr.6.z 16.p.p. na 20.p.p. zostanie ogłoszoną przez Sztab Główny w najbliższym czasie.
	Drezyna pancerna	2.dyon p.p.				2		-	5	-	-	-	-	-		60000	-	-	-	20	100		
Nr.7. "Piłsud- czyk"	Dca poc.panc. z poczt.i druż.adm.	2 dyon p.p.						27	8	-	4	-	27	54	35		-	2160	120	80	48	24	-	
	Plut.ogniowe I/7. i II/7.	- " -	4	10				46	2	-	-	-	46	92	48	jak wyżej	300000	3680	-	-	192	96	-	
	Plut.szturmowy	12.p.p.				2		25	3	-	29	25	50	28		60000	3000	-	-	112	56	-	
	" techniczny	1.baon most.kol.						14	1	-	-	14	28	15		-	1120	-	-	-	-	-	
Nr.9. "I.Marsza- łek"	Dca poc.panc. z poczt.i druż.adm.	2 dyon p.p.						27	8	-	4	-	27	54	35		-	2160	120	80	48	24	-	
	Plut.ogniowe I/9. i II/9.	- " -	4	10				46	2	-	-	-	46	92	48	jak wyżej	300000	3680	-	-	192	96	-	
	Plut.szturmowy	16.p.p.				2		25	3	-	29	25	50	28		60000	3000	-	-	112	56	-	
	" techniczny	1.baon most.kol.						14	1	-	-	14	28	15		-	1120	-	-	-	-	-	
Nr.10. "Bartosz Głowacki"	Dca poc.panc. z poczt.i druż.adm.	2 dyon p.p.						27	8	-	4	-	27	54	35		-	2160	120	80	48	24	-	
	Plut.ogniowe I/10. i II/10.	- " -	4	10				46	2	-	-	-	46	92	48	jak wyżej	300000	3680	-	-	192	96	-	
	Plut.szturmowy	1.p.s.p.				2		25	3	-	29	25	50	28		60000	3000	-	-	112	56	-	
	" techniczny	1.baon most.kol.						14	1	-	-	14	28	15		-	1120	-	-	-	-	-	
Dyon zap.poc.panc.N.2.	Drużyna dcy dyonu	2 dyon						6	33	-	-	-	6	6	39	Zapasu mob.nie prze-widuje się.	-	240	-	-	-	-	-	
	Kompanja zapasowa	poc.						21	5	-	-	21	21	5	-		-	840	-	-	-	-	-	
	Poc.panc.szkolny		4	4	1			34	8	-	4	34	34	42		8500	1360	-	-	-	-	-	
Razem:			24	54	4	11		621	116	10	24	145	621	1181	737	W zależności od typu i ilości dział obecnie posiadanych.	1928500	52240	600	400	1800	900	200	
Mat.uzbr.do wykorzystania przez D.O.K.,zgodnie z zał.Nr.4.			13	4		96	6	12	450	78	-	24	162	450	1092	624	1560 2340 600 200	333000	49440	720	480	2388	1194	-
Brak:									171	38	10	-	171	89	113	-	-	2800	-	-	-	-	200
Nadwyżka:			-	-		2	1		-	-	-	17	-	-	-	-	-	-	120	80	588	294	-

A regulation inventory list of armament, ammunition and equipment distribution to individual armoured trains.

bat wagons were renovated, some were rebuilt, the armament was unified, assault wagons were provided with radio communication equipment, and the trains were assigned the reconnaissance draisine platoons R tank rail carriers and TK rail guides (with either TK-3 or TKS tankette). The 2nd Armoured Train Group retained two "Tatra" draisines, previously used in P.P. 5 "Śmiały" and P.P. 6 "Groźny".

The procedure of locomotive exchange begun in 1927 was, for all practical purposes, finalized in the beginning of 1930's. In May of 1931 the 2nd Armoured Train Group had the following Ti3 engines: number 2 (arrived from Jabłonna, previously assigned to "Sosnkowski"); number 4 (replaced the Ti4-180); number 9; number 10; number 13 and an un-armoured Ti3-6 (later exchanged for Ti3-14 from the 1st Armoured Train Group).

The significant deficiency of the 2nd Armoured Train Group was a very limited workshop capability. The routine repairs and conservation of equipment could be carried out by the Group, but more complicated undertakings had to be outsourced to the P.K.P. workshops in Kraków and Nowy Sącz, or, in some instances, had to be conducted by much better equipped facilities at the 1st Armoured Train Group.

The lack of adequate space of the railroad sidings resulted in the fact that the Group could only maintain a limited number of supply wagons. Some 30 covered goods wagons series *Kd*, 7 flat railcars (5 series *Pdks* and two *Pddk*) and 4 passenger wagons series *Dy* (used as officer's sleeping quarters).

The combat trains of the 2nd Armoured Train Group, just like in the 1st Group, were assigned the mobilization numbers in 1939. The code was identical – as they were mobilized at the V Corps District (*Okręg Korpusu V* – Kraków) the first digit was 5 followed by 1 through 5 signifying the order of mobilisation.

An interior of the mechanical workshop, nicknamed "locomotive shed" at Niepołomice base in 1935. The Renault FT (to be more precise, the CWS soft steel training version) and one of the prototype tank rail transporters is seen in the photograph.

Armoured Train P.P. 51
(P.P. 9 "I. Marszałek")

The P.P. 9 "*Marszałek*", the active train of the *2. Dywizjon*, was mobilised as Armoured Train Number 51 (the alternate name versions "*I-Marszałek*", "*I. Marszałek*" and "*Pierwszy Marszałek*" as in "Fist Marshall" were also used). During peacetime it was stationed at the sidings at Cracow-Bonarka. Captain Leon Cymborski remained its commanding officer, while the adjutant of the 2nd Armoured Train Group and the commander of the signals platoon of the Group, Captain Zdzisław Stanisław Rokossowski became the 2nd-in-Command.

A training exercise of the P.P. 51 "Marszałek" at the Podbrodzie station in 1938. The flat railcar is an ordinary Pdks, while the assault wagon 46022 comes form the configuration of the P.P. 53 "Śmiały".

"Marszałek" on the move. Again, in place of its own, a larger assault wagon from "Śmiały" is being used. The flat railcar partially visible to the left has a unique compartment on its bed. The railcar may be spotted in other photographs of the era with different trains. Photo dating to 1937 – 1938.

Both photographs depict "Marszałek" during training at Pilawa in 1934.

Locomotive

The train had *Ti3* locomotive No. 2 with the *12C1* tender Number 428. Manufactured by Hanomag in 1904, its German number was 4024 Danzig (factory number 4117). The locomotive initially served in Legionowo in the *1. Dywizjon* as an engine of the "*Generał Sosnkowski*". After the "*Zagończyk*" and "*Stefan Czarniecki*" trains were disbanded and the rolling stock elements were exchanged between the two units, the *Ti3-2* was transferred to Cracow-Bonarka, and assigned to Armoured Train Number 9 "*I. Marszałek*".

The engineers cab and a fragment of the tender of the Ti3-2 locomotive in 1937.

Locomotive Ti3-2 in 1931.

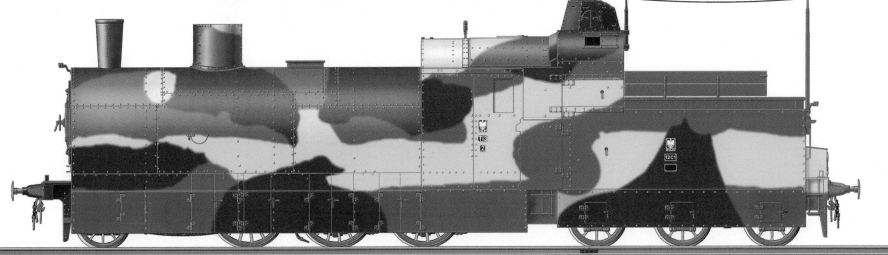

A profile of Ti3-2.

This locomotive, along the G5² locomotive Number 4197, became the standard armouring pattern for all later *Ti3* armoured steam engines (the armour of the locomotive 4197 was removed around 1930, and the locomotive [by that time already designated as *Ti2-73*] was transferred to the civilian authorities; the armour itself was transferred to *Ti3* locomotive Number 3, of "*Generał Sosnkowski*").

A commemorative photograph in front of the artillery wagon, probably from 1934 or 1935.

Preceding page:
P.P. 51 "Marszałek" and the crew in autumn of 1938. It was a common practice to use larger assault wagons during longer exercises; in this case the wagon comes from the rolling stock of "Piłsudczyk".

At the beginning of the 1930's, the command post on *12C1* tender Number 428 was rebuilt – an octagonal "*Ursus*" type turret was installed in place of a typical cylindrical observation post (after the production of *wz. 29* [commonly referred to as "*Ursus*" – name of the manufacturing facility] armoured cars was discontinued, there were about twenty already completed and now surplus turrets – three were used in the *2. Dywizjon* to rebuild the command posts on locomotive tenders).

Artillery Wagons

The "*Marszałek*" had two identical artillery wagons. They were given numbers numbers 460022 and 460023. The wagons were part of the Bolshevik armoured train *BP No.21* "*Imeni Shaumian i Japaridze*" captured on 26 April 1920 by troops of the *51. Kresowy Pułk Piechoty* (51st Borderlands Infantry Regiment). At first, the train was called "*Strzelec Kresowy 13. Dywizji Piechoty*" (Borderlands Rifleman of the 13th Division), later renamed the "*Pierwszy Marszałek Polski, Piłsudski*" (First Marshal of Poland, Piłsudski), and given the number P.P. 21. As the armoured rolling stock was reorganized into six groups with two trains each, the wagons were distributed between "*Bartosz Głowacki*" and "*I. Marszałek*". During subsequent reorganization, into two armoured train groups, they were reunited again in one train.

The wagons were of the so-called "*Sormovo*" type – they were built at the *Krasnoye Sormovo* plant in Nizhny Novgo-

Artillery wagon of "Marszałek" painted in a camouflage pattern in 1934.

Year 1938, "Marszałek" during manoeuvres in Podbrodzie.

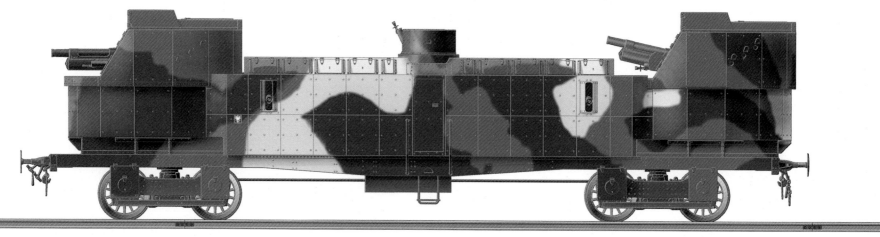

A profile of the artillery wagon number 460022.

"Marszałek" during exercises in September of 1938.

Another photograph from the same exercises.

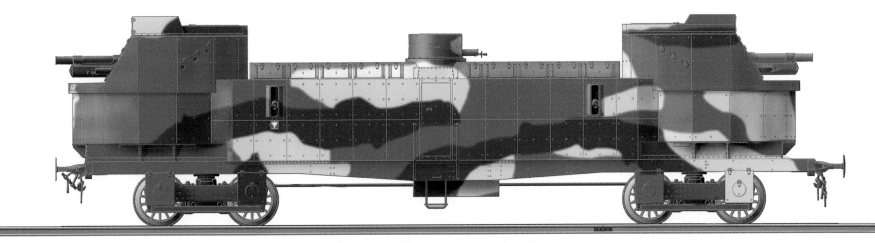

A profile of the artillery wagon number 460023.

rod. This was an exceptionally successful design, not without reason recognised as the best one that was built in Russia.

The train was converted into standard, European gauge in mid-August 1920. The width did exceed the Polish and German rolling stock clearance gauge but it still was within the building clearance gauge, albeit by a very small margin. Due to those clearance concerns, the armoured covers of the wheel axle grease-boxes were later modified by introducing a slight taper towards the inside. The entrance steps also had to be reworked. Other modifications to the wagons were not related to the clearance gauge. The wagons, just like the others, received standard Polish anti-aircraft heavy machine gun turrets.

The 3-inch cannons, which were the original armament of artillery wagons, were the so-called *Lender* guns – the anti-aircraft version of the Russian 3-inch field gun. They were replaced by 75 mm *wz. 02/26* guns – but only new barrels and sights were installed, leaving the Lender mounts unchanged. There were also changes to the chassis – the mechanical brakes were removed and Westinghouse air brakes fitted. The air reservoir and its gear were covered with steel aprons.

"Marszałek" at rest. The artillery turrets are covered with canvas tarpaulins. In the background, an assault wagon form "Śmiały", probably photographed in 1937.

Assault Wagon

It had the number 393088 and was a wagon of the Austro-Hungarian armoured train taken over by Polish troops in Cracow-Prokocim. Its original number was 140866. Previously, the wagon was part of the disbanded "*Stefan Czarniecki*", and prior to that, during the Polish – Bolshevik War, it served in P.P. 1 "*Piłsudczyk*". It was well armoured – the outer armour was 12 mm thick, then there was a 4 cm layer of wood, and some time later, 8 mm of additional internal layer of armour was fitted. The wagon re-

tained its original silhouette with a characteristic observation turret on the roof and the braking system was not converted into an air operated one, but the interior was altered. An inner wireless set compartment and outside masts with extended antenna were installed. The recessed heavy machine gun ports were replaced with retractable sponsons.

The ex-Austrian wagons were comparatively small thus cramped (wheelbase 3,6 m, length of the under-frame 6,8 m), so at the time when the "*Marszałek*" was used for training, an assault wagon from "*Piłsudczyk*" was typically used instead, as it offered more space and comfort.

Preceding page: A "Sormovo" type artillery turret of "Marszałek".
Above on the left: A fragment of the artillery turret seen form the assault wagon. Above on the right: Machine gun turret atop the artillery wagon. On the left: A machine gun, retractable sponson of the assault wagon 393088.
The door panel is ajar but the plates are folded as in closed position.

Side view of the assault wagon 393088.

A photograph of the assault wagon 393088.

Combat Flat Railcars

These were flat railcars of the standard *Pdks* series, with a loading length of 13 m – there were no converted flat cars in the unit with stowage, such as those made in the *1.Dywizjon* from Legionowo. During the mobilisation, the flat railcars from the unit's resources were most likely used in the P.P.51. According to one account, the train would have in its combat section not the regulation set of two, but three flat railcars (in peacetime however, when it was performing exercises, it would have travelled with two). They were ex-German *C143* or nearly identical Polish production *C-VIII* type flat railcars. During the September Campaign, a 40 mm anti-aircraft gun, found on an abandoned transport on 11 September, was placed on one of the wagons.

Draisine Platoon

Standard composition of two *R* draisines – *Renault FT* tank on rail transporter, four *TK* draisines – *TK-3* tankette on rail guides and one *TK-3* as a spare (it is not known whether carried on a flat railcar in the combat section or in the administrative section).

Administrative Supply Train Section

The administrative section, similarly to the combat train, was formed before the outbreak of the war to the typical assembly standards. It is possible that some of the wagons of the administrative section were the unit's own rolling

A profile of the flat railcar Pdks with the 40 mm anti-aircraft cannon.

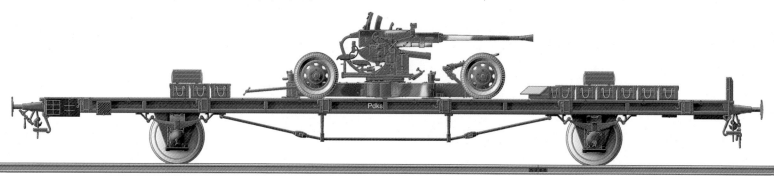

stock, and there is even a report that all the wagons were from the resources of the *2. dywizjon*. The motor vehicle types assigned to the train are unknown, but a *Polski Fiat 508 "Łazik"* was documented to be among them. The locomotive was delivered by the *DOKP Kraków* (National Railways Regional Authority – Cracow) it is quite likely that it was *Tr11* (there were several dozen of these in the Cracow railways district, and 145 in the entire *P.K.P.* – they were familiar and used in the railway troops from the time of the war with the Bolsheviks, and it is certain that the administrative sections of the *"Śmiały"* as well as *"Piłsudczyk"* received these engines as well).

"I. Marszałek" in September 1939

The train completed its mobilisation process on 27 August at the Skawina station, where it was dispatched to relief the already congested Cracow-Bonarka railroad sidings. Part of the original crew was reassigned the remaining trains of the formation, and supplemented by the reservists. The mobilized train was at the disposal of the *Armia "Kraków"* ("Cracow" Army).

On 1 September 1939 the train was ordered to move towards Chabówka, to patrol the Osielec-Jordanów section of the tracks, and to support the troops of the *1. Brygada Górska* (1st Mountain Brigade) with its gunfire. In the afternoon, German troops at the Spytkowice Pass and on the Obidowa ridge were shelled by the train from the vicinity of Jordanów.

On 2 September, the train remained at the Jordanów station. In the morning, during artillery barrage directed at the station, the commander of the train, Captain Cymborski, was wounded, and his post was taken over by Captain Rokossowski. For the next several hours, the train bombarded German troops with fire directed by Lieutenant Kazimierz Pfaffenhofen-Chłędowski from a forward observation post (or perhaps from a tankette), supporting the actions of *10. Brygada Kawalerii* (10th Cavalry Brigade). During an artillery duel with German batteries, between 15:00 and 16:00 hours the observation post was hit and Lieutenant Pfaffenhofen-Chłędowski was wounded. Attempts were made to control the fire from the set of armoured draisines *TK-R-TK* using radio communications (one *R* draisine was supposedly knocked out in this action near Chabówka, but this is not confirmed by other reports). At around 17:00 hours, the commander of the reconnaissance group of the *10. Brygada Kawalerii* announced that he was retreating in the direction of the

Locomotive Ti3-2 – photograph taken by NKVD after the train was captured by the Soviets.

Zakopane-Kraków road so the train departed to the Sucha station, where it was ordered to withdraw to Skawina.

On 4 September the P.P. 51 was to perform reconnaissance mission in the direction of Zator (near Oświęcim). However, as it seems, only the *TK-R-TK* draizine set went out to scout, because the train required maintenance. In the interim, pending further orders, it was possible to replenish supplies and perform a routine steam boiler flush. Captain Rokossowski went by a *PF 508 "Łazik"* to Cracow, where he learned that the *Armia "Kraków"* was retreating to the east – therefore he decided to send the train to Kraków-Płaszów and then to Tarnów.

The route to Tarnów was extremely difficult – many times it was necessary to remove the wreckage, push disabled transport trains out of the way, and repair damaged tracks and bypasses. The train arrived in Tarnów on 6 September, where information was recieved that it was Dębica which was designated as the concentration point for the troops retreating from Cracow. An air raid damaged the tracks ahead – the crew had to carry out a repair – so the train only arrived in Dębica on 7 September. P.P 51 managed to survive German air assault on Dębica without any damage. Updated information about the grouping of General Boruta-Spiechowicz's units in Mielec forced the train move on. On 8 September, without any major problems, the train reached Mielec, and then travelled further, because new information was received that troops

After it was captured, "Marszałek" assault wagon received number ŻBO-023 (ЖБО – ZhBO – railway armoured vehicle).

Artillery wagon pressed in service by NKVD as ŻBO-108.

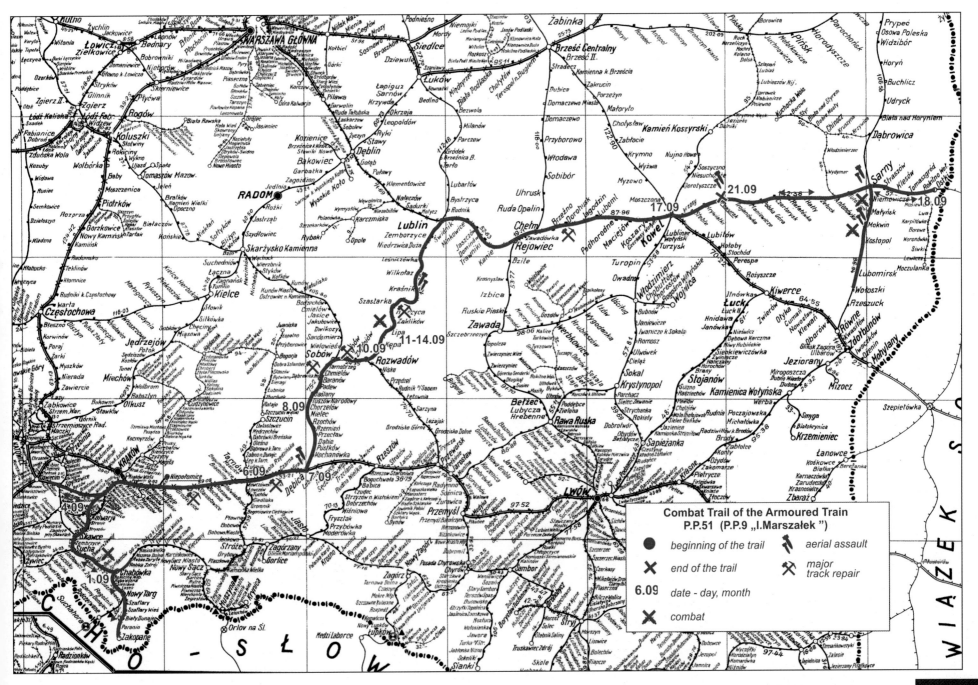

**Combat Trail of the Armoured Train
P.P.51 (P.P.9 „I.Marszałek ")**

● beginning of the trail   ⚒ aerial assault

✕ end of the trail   ⚒ major track repair

6.09 date - day, month

✕ combat

were actually concentrating between Tarnobrzeg and Rozwadów. Movement was very difficult because the tracks were obstructed by evocation trains.

On 9 September P.P. 51 passed through Tarnobrzeg without a halt. The line to Rozwadów was again blocked by wrecked or abandoned evacuation trains so the crew had to work all day, removing the damaged wagons from the tracks. Finally, on 10 September, the P.P. 51 got to the now ruined junction in Rozwadów.

At the Rozwadów station, the train's crew aided in assembling of a medical transport echelon, composed of random wagons and coaches, which – filled with the wounded, was sent to Lublin.

On the night of 10 – 11 September, the train was used to deliver food and ammunition from Zaklików station to Kępa station. On 11 September, the train crew found an abandoned 40 mm anti-aircraft gun at the *Rozwadów Towarowa* (Stalowa Wola township) station, which was placed on a flat railcar to strengthened the anti-aircraft defences of the train.

On 12 September, the P.P. 51 train was sent to cover the bridge crossing over the San River near the village of Kępa. On 14 September, at dawn, after the bridge was blown up by engineers, the train set off for Lublin. Halfway, at Szastarka, the armoured train survived a heavy air raid – the equipment did not suffer any damage, but the transport trains travelling ahead were destroyed. Wreckage had to be removed and the tracks repaired. From

Photograph from November of 1941. The artillery wagon in German hands – "betreten verboten" chalk marking translates into "do not enter".

Lublin, the train was sent back west to Zaklików again. From the morning of 15 September it supported the ground units.

Late on 15 September the train arrived again at Lublin, where it was decided to travel to Lwów (Lviv) via Rejowiec. It turned out that the Rejowiec-Lviv tracks were blocked by rolling stock along its entire length all of the way to Rawa Ruska, and the only clear route led through Chełm to Kowel and then probably through Włodzimierz Wołyński. En route, it was once more necessary to push the wreckage off the line and repair the tracks. In Kowel, on 16 September, the further journey through Włodzimierz turned out to be impossible, and it was also impossi-

ble to go through Kiwerce. The only route left open led to Sarny, at which the train arrived in the evening.

Upon arrival, the Regional Commander at Sarny dispatched the P.P. 51 for reconnaissance in the direction of Równe. Soviet armour was spotted advancing towards the town. The train, as instructed, did not open fire (to remain neutral or passive, towards the Soviet units was the general directive at the time) and attempted to pull back towards Sarny. However, an exchange of fire with the Soviets eventually took place near Kostopol. Most likely, four armoured cars, three tractors and a few other Soviet vehicles were knocked out in the course of the skirmish.

A raid by Soviet planes at 10:00 hours caused a lot of damage to the area surrounding the train, but with a worthy response – one of the attacking *R-5* light bombers was shot down (according to another report it was an *SB-2* medium bomber plane). Afterwards the train was patrolling near Sarny, occasionally firing at Russian planes and some cavalry troops in support the *KOP* (*Korpus Ochrony Pogranicza* – Border Protection Corps) soldiers near Niemowice. On 20 September, there were no more Polish troops defending Sarny, so Captain Rokossowski made the decision to return to Kowel.

In the afternoon of 21 September 1939, the train reached the Powórsk station where it got stuck with no ability

Armoured wagons of "Marszałek" captured by the Germans sitting on the railroad siding in 1941

Armoured locomotive of "Marszałek" in German hands in 1941.

to advance or withdraw. Ukrainian independence rebels (partisan units, but also ordinary thug gangs) became a threat, but it was stopped by the firm response of the train's crew. In the late afternoon, the train was bombed by Soviet planes. Both the armoured train and its administrative section were damaged, so the commanding officer, Captain Rokossowski, ordered the train to be abandoned. There is another account, contrary to the one provided by Captain Rokossowski, where the author claims that the train was not damaged but simply deserted due to the advance of Soviet troops which cut off the route to Lwów.

After leaving the train, some of the crew under the command of Captain Rokosowski joined the KOP Group of General Orlik-Rückeman as an infantry unit called "Pociąg Pancerny nr. 51".

After the battle of Wytyczno, the unit joined the *Grupa Operacyjna "Polesie"* (Operational Group), which carried on the fight and eventually surrendered after the battle of Kock on 6 October 1939 as the last Polish Army unit in the field.

The train was seized by Soviet troops and, after repairs, pressed in service as the *Broneepoyezd –* (armoured train [*BP* or *BEPO* for short]) of the – 77th NKVD Regiment (*Naródnyy komissariát vnútrennikh del –* People's Commissariat for Internal Affairs). The assault wagon was marked as *Zheleznodorozhny Bronirowanny Obyekt No 023 –* armoured railway item (*ZhBO-023*; it is possible that it was excluded from the combat composition of the reactivated train), artillery wagon 460022 as *ZhBO-108*, artillery wagon 460023 as *ZhBO-109*, and the locomotive – *ZhBO-107*. In June 1941, the train

was stationed in Stanisławów (renamed Ivano-Frankivsk). After the German attack on 22 June 1941, the train supported its retreating parent regiment. On 5 July 1941 it fought with German tanks, destroying or damaging several of them according to Soviet sources. On 7 July it was abandoned by the crew.

The train was taken over by the Germans; over a next few months it was refurbished, rebuilt and re-commissioned in December 1941. The Germans formed the powerful *Panzerzug PZ.10* armoured train out of two former Polish trains captured by the Soviets. *PZ.10* consisted of two parts: *Kampfzug A* (also known as *PZ.10a*; former P.P. 53 "Śmiały"; *BEPO* of the 75th NKVD Regiment) and *Kampfzug B* (*PZ.10b*; former P.P. 51 "Marszałek"; *BEPO* of the 77th NKVD Regiment). The *Panzerzug 10b* had both

"Marszałek's" artillery wagons and initially also its *Ti3-2* armoured locomotive. In June 1942, the train received new infantry (assault) wagons and a German locomotive. Throughout all its service the train was used on the Eastern Front and was damaged several times.

On 31 July 1943, *Panzerzug 10* was divided into two separate trains. *Kampfzug A* (former P.P. 53) remained under the name *PZ.10*, while *Kampfzug B* (former P.P. 51) was renamed *Panzerzug 11*. In the summer of 1944 *Panzerzug 11* took part in delaying actions and finally, at the end of 1944, it operated in the Kielce region. The ex-"Marszałek" ended its combat career on 13 January 1945 near Chęciny. The train was abandoned due to the destruction of the bridge over the Nida River; it could not retreat any further.

"Marszałek" *pressed into service by the Germans as Pz.10b.*

Armoured Train P.P. 52
(P.P. 7 "Piłsudczyk")

The P.P. 7 "*Piłsudczyk*", previously used as an excercise train, was mobilised as Armoured Train Number 52. On 26 August 1939, Captain Mikołaj Gonczar, its peacetime commander, was retained as a commanding officer, and his second-in-command became Lieutenant Bolesław Sitkowski, who was previously leading the signals platoon in the *2. Dywizjon*. The train was assigned to the *30. Dywizja Piechoty* (30th Division) of the *Armia "Łódź"*.

Celebration of the 2. Dywizjon Pociągów Pancernych (2nd Armoured Train Group) holiday, in Niepołomice – behind the troops at attention, a field altar is visible in front of the "Piłsudczyk" armoured train.

Photographs taken probably in 1935; P.P. 52 "Piłsudczyk" during exercises. There is an unusual sequence of equipment, the locomotive is in the rear pushing the armoured wagons. The Pdks flat railcar has a unique compartment on the top of the cargo bed – seen previously in the composition of "Marszałek".

A profile of the Ti3-13 *locomotive.*

Locomotive

Ti3 Number 13 with tender *12C1* Number 481, of Hohenzollern production in 1905, German number 4022 Frankfurt (factory number 1773). In the early 1930's, the command post on tender No. 481 was rebuilt. Instead of a cylindrical observation turret, an octagonal "*Ursus*" type turret was fitted.

2. Dywizjon Pociągów Pancernych *during summer exercises in the vicinity of Pilawa in 1934 – the* Ti3-13 *locomotive hauls* Pdks *flat railcars.*

In the background, the Ti3-13 may be seen – still in an overall gray paint scheme. The photograph was taken in early 1930's before the alterations to the engineer's cab entrance and the commander's post on the tender. The identification markings are still painted. They were eventually replaced by cast metal plaques.

Locomotive Ti3-13 and its crew around 1935.

A commemorative photograph taken in front of the artillery wagon of "Piłsudczyk" around year 1935.

"Piłsudczyk" during the Divisional holiday, probably in 1938.

An officer of the KOP – Korpus Ochrony Pogranicza *(Border Protection Corps) visiting the 2. Dywizjon on the motorcycle. In the background,* Kd *covered wagons of the supply echelons followed by artillery wagons of "Piłsudczyk" and* "Marszałek". *Note the tarpaulins covering the turrets. Circa 1937.*

Artillery wagons

Two identical wagons with the numbers 699069 and 699070. These were of Polish construction from the Cegielski Plant, the so-called Type III. They were built on the chassis of German heavy flat railcars for rail transport. Type III was a technical advancement over the Type II design. A minor fault – the cannon turret located too high, was altered. The wagon crew compartment was symmetrical, lowered under the cannon turret, just as it was under the howitzer turret. This reduced the significant drawback – rocking of the wagon when firing. The overall height of the casemate central section was increased about 20 cm – not a lot, but compared to the Type II it improved the conditions for the crew as the internal height of 175 cm allowed most of the crew members to stand up straight. The turrets, nearly identical with type II, were previously assessed as practical and comfortable, even though the entry was deemed somewhat difficult. The semi-barrel profile of the armour only to some extent made it difficult for a projectile to pierce the steel, and it reduced the already modest internal space of the wagon. The sides were upright, almost a metre high so they did offer the deflecting properties.

Both profiles – artillery wagon 699069 shown from the left and the right.

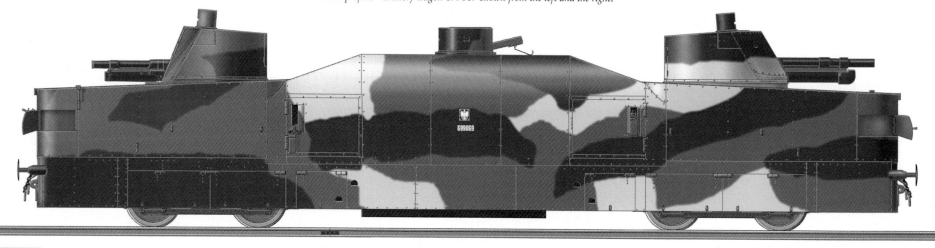

On the left: A sporting event photographed in front of the artillery wagon; around 1935. Below: The participants posing in front of the assault wagon. On the right: Front view of the artillery wagon 699069.

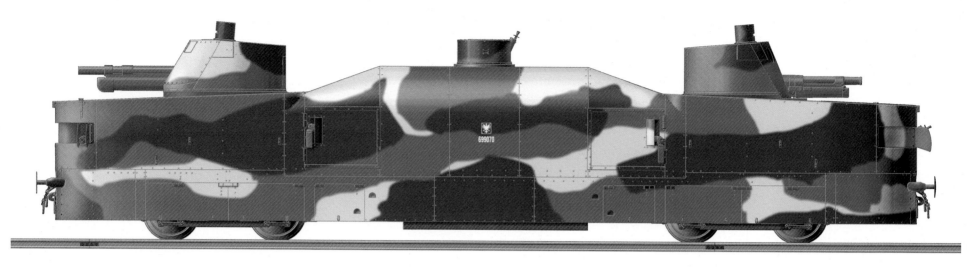

A profile of the artillery wagon 699070.

Side view of the artillery wagon 699069 with partially extended machine gun sponsons.

Assault wagon 402633.

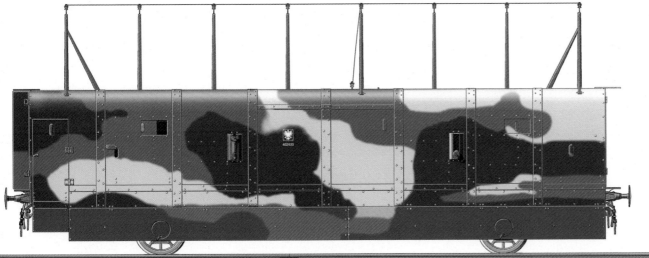

A profile of the assault wagon 402633.

Assault wagon

This had the number 402633 and was built on the chassis of a *Jk* series Austro-Hungarian open coal wagon. It was originally an artillery wagon with a cannon turret on the roof. This early design with the gun placed high above the track, and therefore with a high centre of gravity, was prone to rocking so there were problems with accuracy during rapid firing, because the oscillation faded out quite slowly. Almost all artillery wagons of this sort were converted into assault versions.

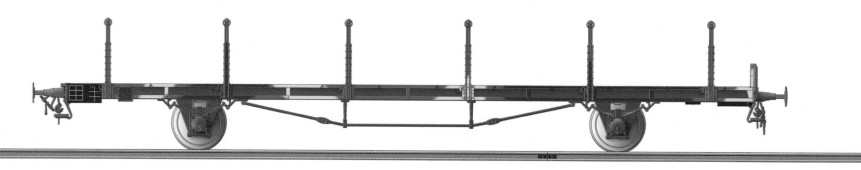

Profiles of the Pdks flat railcars – in 1939 both had a camouflage pattern paint.

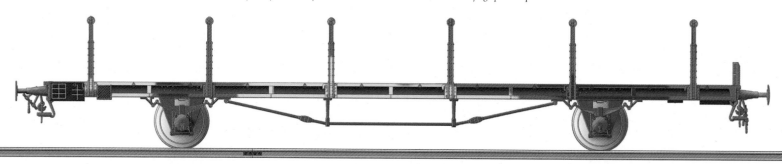

Combat Flat Railcars

Both flat railcars were of the *Pdks* standard series, with a loading length of 13 m. They were ex-German *C143* flat railcars or an equivalent Polish production *C-VIII* type. It is not known whether the *"Piłsudczyk"* administrative section included flat railcars provided by *P.K.P.* or from the unit's divisional resources. It is also possible that there were three and not two flat railcars in the combat section of the train – the three according to only one report, which, however, contains so many inconsistencies that it cannot be trusted without reservations.

Draisine platoon

The regulation two sets of draisines *TK-R-TK* and a spare tankette with a spare rail guide. All *TKS* tankettes, but only two of them

Administrative Supply Train Section

"Black" locomotive series *Tr11* (Austrian Series *kkStB 170*) and wagons delivered by *P.K.P.* The composition was probably in line with the regulations – except for an addition of a workshop wagon. Among the wheeled equipment – cer-

tainly a motorcycle and a *Polski Fiat 508 "Łazik"*. An information about forming the echelon from own rolling stock of the 2. *Dywizjon* cannot be true – the number of carriages of the unit allowed to form only one regular administrative supply train, so either *"Marszałek"* had divisional rolling stock, and then there were not enough for *"Piłsudczyk"*, or vice versa.

"Piłsudczyk" in September 1939

On the evening of 28 August, at the siding in Podłęże, the train was assembled with draisines and rail guides on flat rail-

cars. The steam locomotive was flushed out and coal was also loaded in Podłęże. The "black" *Tr11* locomotive intended for the administrative echelon had already arrived. The train left Podłęże on the same night with an order to go to Koluszki, the destination changed at the last minute to Zduńska Wola. Finally, in the evening of the following day, it entered the station at Siemkowice, which was assigned as a stand-by station instead of Zduńska Wola as the latter was no longer operational. In the morning, the draisines were set up onto the tracks and the train set off towards Działoszyn to get acquainted with the route along the area of possible future operations. A collision with the leading draisine set damaged the tankette and its rail guide. The malfunction – a seizing of one artillery wagon's axle forced the train to return to Siemkowice – the wagon was sent with an armoured steam locomotive to Karsznice (near Zduńska Wola); it was the closest available repair facility.

The wagon and the locomotive returned on the morning of 1 September, and resumed their places in the combat formation. At 04:30 hours, P.P. 53 "Śmiały" entered the station. Some time later, a German plane appeared over the area, and was fired at by the heavy machine gun of the "Piłsudczyk" without any noticable effects. Captain Gonczar ordered fire to cease because the news that war had already begun did not reached the train yet.

Around 10 o'clock, "Śmiały" left for Miedzno, and a short time later "Piłsudczyk" left as well, stopping in Działoszyn. In the meantime, there was an air attack on Siemkowice, but luckily the administrative sections of both trains did not suffer any damage. In the afternoon, the commanding officer of the *30. Dywizja Piechoty* boarded the "Piłsudczyk" and ordered a move towards the sounds of gunfire in the sector of front held by the *Wołyńska Brygada Kawalerii* (Volhynian Cavalry Brigade). The communications were disrupted so the situation had to be clarified as soon as possible. The train reached Miedzno at the most opportune moment – its fire significantly supported "Śmiały", which had been engaging German tanks since the morning.

"Piłsudczyk" derailed at Mrozy. Both photographs depict the train seen from the rear.

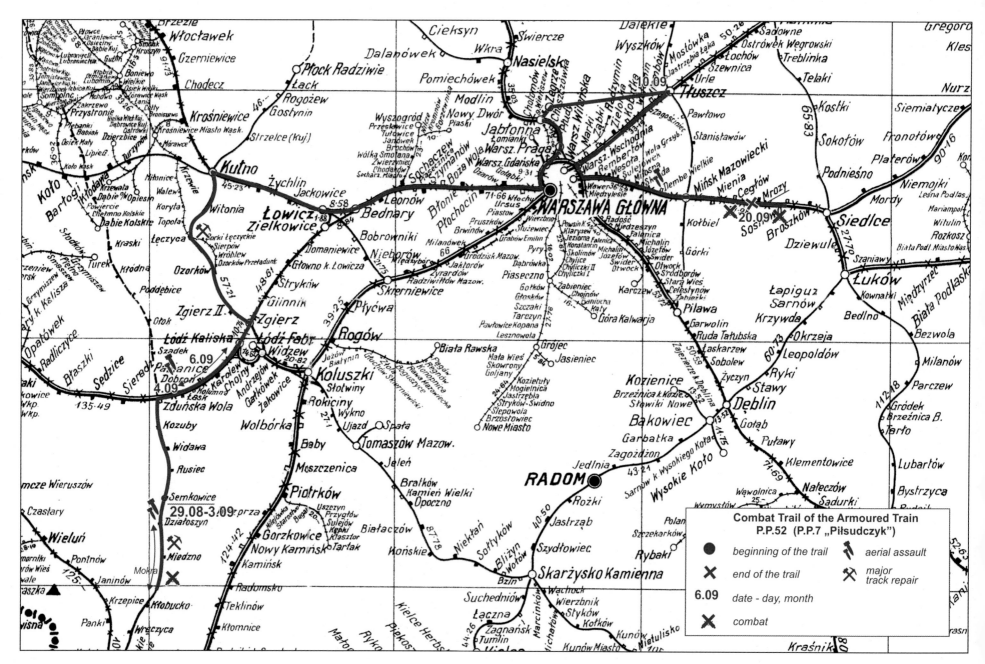

Combat Trail of the Armoured Train
P.P.52 (P.P.7 „Piłsudczyk")

- ● beginning of the trail
- ✕ end of the trail
- 6.09 date - day, month
- ✕ combat
- ⚒ aerial assault
- ⚒ major track repair

Combat route of armoured train "Piłsudczyk" in 1939.

Derailed "Piłsudczyk" and German sappers building a detour track.

Armoured locomotive of "Piłsudczyk".

Rear artillery wagon after removal of the flat railcar.

After the action both trains withdrew towards Działoszyn, but they could not reach Siemkowice because German air raid had broken the tracks. The repairs, carried out by both crews and the local civilian population, lasted until dawn.

In the morning in Siemkowice, the tankette that had been damaged the previous night was loaded onto a flat railcar and sent with an administrative steam engine to Karsznice (there is no clarity here – if the draisines were coupled in a regular manner, and were ran over by a flat railcar so badly that the tankette was damaged, the impact should have had demolished the rail guide as well, so both, the tankette and the rail guide would need repair; in an unlikely event the guide was pushed off the track, it could have been just the tankette). Captain Gonczar drove from Karsznice to Łódź on a motorcycle taken from the administrative section, but he did not succeed in contacting the HQ of the *Armia "Łódź"* as he intended. The

repaired tankette and the service locomotive were already waiting – so it was possible to return to Siemkowice. Afterwards, the train took part in the fighting near Działoszyn.

3 September passed quite calmly except for some harassing aircraft – it had been proven by then that two anti-aircraft machine guns were only an illusion of a defence. The administrative train was sent to Łask station, while the armoured train went to Widawa and came under the orders of the *28. Dywizja Piechoty* (28th Division).

On 4 September "Piłsudczyk" travelled to Łask. It was ordered to support the infantry counterattack on Mnichów. A tankette fitted for wireless communication was sent ahead with an artillery observer. The artillery fire of the train inflicted heavy losses on the Germans, but the infantry attack was unsuccessful and the train's guns finally covered the retreat of the ground troops. Shortly thereafter,

Another view of the rear of the armoured train.

near Łask, the train became the target of an air attack – it had some wounded in both the combat and administrative sections (the workshop wagon was thrown off the track and overturned), bombs set a nearby ammunition train on fire and destroyed the tracks. The situation became serious and Captain Gonczar ordered the train to be abandoned. It was somehow managed to push away the wagons loaded with ammunition, so when the explosions stopped and the air raid ended, the crew returned to the train. The track damage was so severe that the train appeared lost – but with the great efforts of the crew the repair was carried out – but only a provisional one: in one of the reports we find the following statement: "...the train had no possibility to pass through there, it must have jumped over this section".

On 6 September the P.P. 52 was patrolling between Łask and Łódź, but due to the general retreat it was ordered to withdraw to defend Warsaw. The administrative train set off on the Łódź – Zgierz – Łowicz line, followed by the combat section with a set of draisines coupled to the rear of the train. After a few kilometres, it was necessary to go back to Zgierz, because the rail line, packed with transport trains, offered no chance to travel. Preceded again by the administrative echelon with draisines coupled to the rear flat railcar, "Piłsudczyk" was redirected to the tracks leading to Kutno. Plagued by air raids and forced to repair the tracks along the way, the train reached Łęczyca, where the damage was very substantial – in order to clear the way it was necessary to use welding torches to cut tangled wreckage. At Łęczyca, the train was assigned an additional task – to protect the bank's evacuation train from Poznań. With great difficulties, on 8 September the trains reached the Warsaw-West station, through the ruined Łowicz, and then the Warsaw-Praga station. An order from the Warsaw defence command directed the train to Legionowo, where it received yet another dispatch – to travel to Tłuszcz (an encounter with the P.P. 13 "General Sosnkowski" from the 1. Dywizjon took place in Tłuszcz).

On the same day of 10 September, Captain Gonczar received an order to travel along the Warsaw ring line through Mińsk Mazowiecki to Rembertów, but the line was not passable so the train had to reroute via Wołomin and Warsaw-East, and then from Rembertów to Mińsk Mazowiecki. At the Dębe Wielkie station, a few kilometres before Mińsk, "Piłsudczyk" and its administrative supply train had to halt because of the congestion. They were attacked by planes – firing howitzer shrapnel rounds at high elevation made it possible to shot down one of the aircraft. A close bomb explosion knocked the flat railcar of the combat section off the rails, but the crew managed to put it back on track. During the aerial

Both images show the rear artillery wagon and a fragment of the flat railcar.

assault the steam engine of the administrative section was destroyed so was the tank wagon coupled to it. The *Tr11* engine was hit several times. The boiler was knocked out and the steam engine was pushed of the track. It was replaced by a civilian *Ty23*.

The main cause of the congestion turned out to be the lack of water at the Mińsk Mazowiecki station – the crew managed to get the station pump working (it had clear signs of sabotage) and the traffic jam was slowly dissolving.

While setting off, the train ran over the rail carrier with the *R* tank – destroying both – they had to be pushed off the track.

Travelling in the direction of Siedlce, the trains took the left track because the right one was completely impassable. As it was impossible to continue movement to Mrozy, the railway engineers from the evacuation transport built a bypass crossing to the left track from dismantled rails – the combat section continued towards Siedlce. The tankette sent for reconnaissance reported that there were already Germans in Siedlce. On the same day in the evening, the Germans captured Mińsk Mazowiecki, so the trains found themselves sacked – the administrative section in the siding at Mrozy, and the combat section farther east with manoeuvrability possibilities but only to a minimal extent.

A strong impromptu defensive group was created from the crews of evacuation trains (there was a train with engineers from the *2. Batalion Mostów Kolejowych*, an evacuation train of "balloonists" from Legionowo, a train with cadets and aviation officers) and from random infantry and field gun batteries. Armoured train "Piłsudczyk" became an important element of the defence, although it was necessary to heat the boiler using railroad ties – every second railway sleeper was extracted from under nearby tracks.

On 20 September, having only one operational cannon with six rounds of ammunition and three functioning machine guns left on the train, the group commander decided to abandon the defences and break through the encirclement. The engineers blew up a piece of the rail track; the engine driver put the train in motion so it consequently derailed.

The Germans managed to refurbish the locomotive, artillery wagon number 699069 and the assault wagon and press them in service. In June 1940, an artillery wagon and a steam engine from "Piłsudczyk", supplemented the assault wagon of "Groźny" and the artillery wagon from the excersize train, were commissioned as *Panzerzug 21 (Pz. 21)*. The train was in service until October 1944, when it was destroyed near Mažeikiai in Lithuania. The assault wagon from "Piłsudczyk" was assigned to *Panzerzug 22* and remained in service until February 1945, when it was destroyed together with the entire train in Szprotawa.

Photographs show the retractable machine gun sponson – on the left, artillery wagon 699069; on the right 699070

Both photographs:
"Piłsudczyk" still resting on the damaged section of the rails. The detour track is already in place, and the front artillery wagon, as well as both flat railcars was hauled away. But, apparently, there was some sort of a difficulty with moving the rear artillery wagon, assault wagon and the locomotive.

Upper left:
Artillery wagon 699070.

Upper right and opposing:
Artillery wagon 699069 (and an assault wagon) after transfer to some railway depot.

German railway men in front of the Ti3-13 locomotive with the Polish Eagle plaque removed. The Ti3-13 locomotive was for some time stored at the railway siding of Krakow station.

Artillery wagon 699069 from "Piłsudczyk" pulled away from the tracks damaged at Mrozy to some temporary location.

A view of an assault wagon from "Groźny" and the locomotive from "Piłsudczyk" – with the command turret removed.

Winter of 1940 – artillery wagon 699069 of "Piłsudczyk" at the railway siding of Krakow station.

Panzerzug 21 – *artillery wagon of "Piłsudczyk", assault wagon from "Groźny" and the locomotive of "Piłsudczyk".*

Armoured Train P.P. 53 (P.P. 5 "Śmiały")

Armoured Train Number 5 "Śmiały", held in the so-called MOB stock (mobilisation reserve), was mobilised in Cracow-Bonarka in August 1939 as Armoured Train 53 (P.P. 53). Captain Mieczysław Malinowski was appointed as the commanding officer; the post of the second-in-command was taken up by Lieutenant Wacław Elertowicz. The train was assigned to the *Wołyńska Brygada Kawalerii* (Volhynian Cavalry Brigade).

Year 1930 – "Śmiały" on a bridge over the Świder River (tributary of Wisła south of Warsaw). The locomotive and wagons are seen before final modifications.

A profile of the Ti3-9 locomotive.

Locomotive

Ti3 number 9 with *12C1* tender with an unknown number (the information that it was tender no. 480 is incorrect – most likely it was no. 482). This steam locomotive was manufactured by the Borsig factory in 1904, German number 4005 Katowitz (factory number 5406). At the beginning of the 1930's, the command post on the tender was rebuilt. Instead of a cylindrical observation turret, an octagonal "*Ursus*" turret was installed.

The crew of "Śmiały" in early 1930's.

"Śmiały" during Divisional exercises in Tłuszcz (near Warsaw) in 1931.

Artillery wagons

Two identical Polish-built Type III wagons with the numbers 699020 and 699021. The wagons were identical to the ones of "Piłsudczyk" – except, of course, for the camouflage pattern, because this was different on each of the wagons. They can also be distinguished by the fact that they had one entry step cut under the sponsons, not two as in the "Piłsudczyk".

Each of these wagons had a 75 mm *wz. 02/26* cannon and a 100 mm *wz. 14/19A* howitzer.

Assault wagon

The wagon was numbered 627950 and it was of the so-called "warsaw" type. The design of this type of combat railcar was developed at the beginning of 1920

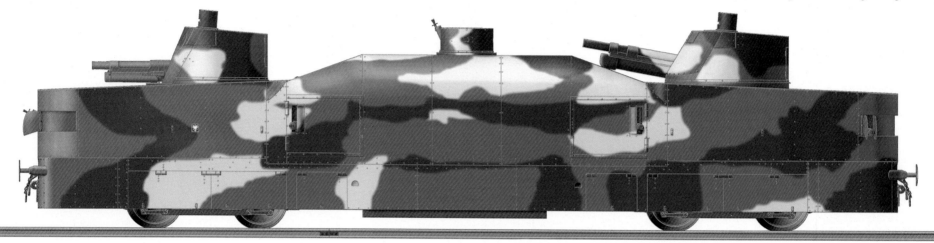

A profiles of "Śmiały" artillery wagons. On the top: wagon 699020; below: wagon 699021.

at the Warsaw branch of *Kierownictwo Budowy Pociągów Pancernych* (Armoured Train Construction Directorate). The armour was applied to typical Tsarist standard flat railcars with a wheelbase of 5,5 m (length of the under-frame 9,2 m) and a load capacity of 1,000 poods, equivalent to 16,380 kg. The armour had a characteristic semi-barrel shape. Originally, the wagon had an observation turret, which was removed during the installation of the wireless set and its external antennae posts. During the reconstruction of the wagon, the side walls were fitted with typical cylindrical heavy machine gun mounts and a double-panel door was installed (previously, the wagon had entrances only in the end walls).

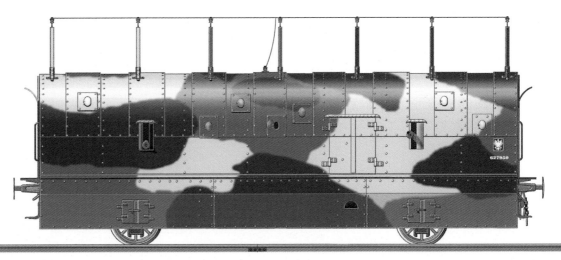

A profile of "Śmiały" assault wagon 627950.

Cropped and enlarged fragment of armoured train "Marszałek" during exercises – longer assault wagon from "Śmiały" was used for convenience.

Side view of the assault wagon from "Śmiały" in its final form after all modifications.

The maintenance of the howitzer, most likely during summer training at Pilawa.

Combat flat railcars

Flat cars of the *Pdks* series, with a loading length of 13 m, were supplied by *P.K.P.* These were ex-German *C143* platforms or the identical C-VIII series, manufactured in Poland.

Draisine platoon

Standard – two R draisine rail transporters, four *TK* (*TK-3* tankette) draisines on rail guides and one *TK* tankette with a guide as a spare.

Administrative Supply Train Section

Consisted of an unarmoured locomotive of the *Tr11* series and wagons provided by the *P.K.P.* – composition probably in line with the regular arrangement.

"Śmiały" in September 1939

In the evening of 25 August or perhaps the 27, the train was completely ready to depart with a platoon of draisines loaded together with their rail guides onto the flat cars, following an order to travel through Cracow and Częstochowa to Koluszki. The route was changed at the last minute to travel from Częstochowa straight to the Siemkowice station. There was probably a reason, such as the late arrival of the order (we will probably never know for certain), that the train passed Częstochowa and continoud towards Koluszki. It reached the Rudniki station, late in the evening of 28 August. Deliberations on how to use the train continued during the night of 30/31 August. The headquarters of the *Wołyńska Brygada Kawalerii* decided to deploy P.P. 53 on the Działoszyn-Herby section of the track, at the first line of defence, while the staff of *Armia "Łódź"* initially suggested the recently built Siemkowice – Częstochowa line, with a stand-by position at the station in Dubidza or Rząsawa, or in between them, in Cykarzewo.

On the night of 31 August – 1 September, already in full combat readiness, P.P. 53 together with its administrative section left Rudniki for Siemkowice, where it arrived in the morning at 04:30 hours. A rendezvous with the P.P. 52 "Piłsudczyk" took place, as the latter had already been in Siemkowice for two days. Before 10 o'clock "Śmiały" set off for Miedzno and took up its stand-by position near the town. Soon after, Siemkowowice was bombed by German planes. During the stopover in Miedzno Captain Malinowski received an order over the radio to join the fighting that had flared up near the village of Mokra. The German *4. Panzer Division* struck the defensive positions of the *Wołyńska Brygada Kawalerii* near Kłobuck with all its might – and it had over three hundred tanks, additionally supported by artillery and aircraft. In the first clash with the *21. Pułk Ułanów* (21st Lancers) manning the centre of the defensive line, the Germans were quickly repulsed. Two hours later, another armoured thrust commenced, straight into the centre of the village of Mokra and the intervention of the armoured train became necessary. The gunfire of the train, carried out from the elevated embankment overlooking the German formation, was very effective and forced the enemy to withdraw.

After this first and extremely effective action, the train probably halted in the railway cutting extending just behind the Mokra – Miedzna road culvert. Taking advantage of the pause in action, the crew improved the field camouflage and dispatched one of the armoured draisines for reconnaissance in the direction of Kłobuck; the scouts soon reported that the enemy had not appeared at Kłobuck so far. Another attack by German tanks, preceded by an artillery barrage and air raids, began around 14:00 hours. The German armour reappeared with strength of around 70 armoured vehicles. The fire of Polish horse artillery cannons, anti-tank guns and anti-tank rifles did not manage to stop the tanks, which penetrat-

Artillery wagon 699021 on a catalogue photograph taken by NKVD. Soviet number ZhBO-195.

Assault wagon (with wheel aprons removed) carried number ZhBO-106.

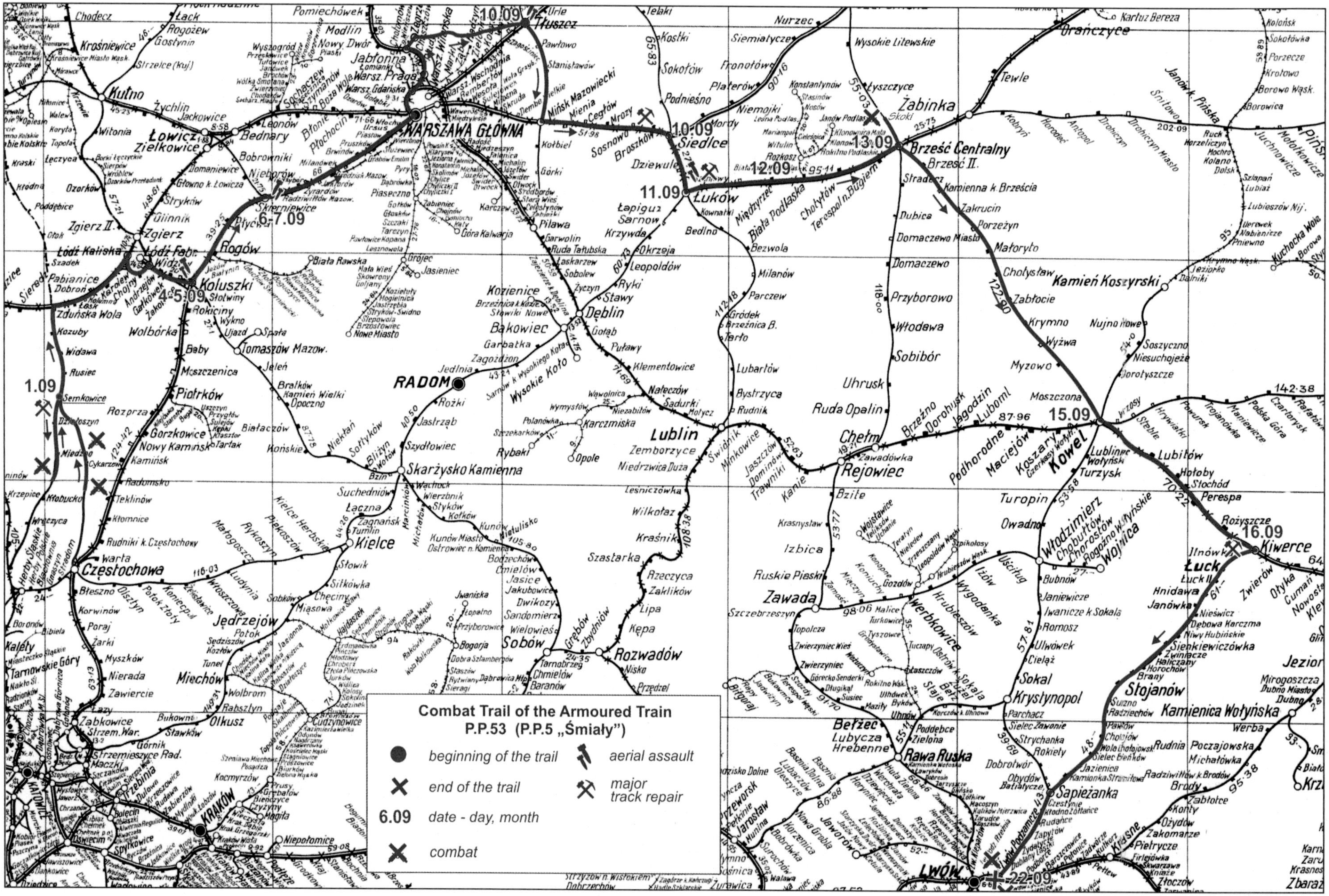
Combat Trail of the Armoured Train
P.P.53 (P.P.5 „Śmiały")
beginning of the trail
aerial assault
end of the trail
major track repair
6.09 date - day, month
combat
1.09
4-5.09
6-7.09
10.09
11.09
12.09
13.09
15.09
16.09
22.09
WARSZAWA GŁÓWNA
RADOM
Lublin
Kowel
Łuck
Kiwerce
Brześć Centralny
Siedlce
Łuków
Koluszki
Częstochowa
Kraków
Kielce
Lwów
Tłuszcz

Combat route of armoured train "Śmiały" in 1939.

ed deeper and deeper. "*Śmiały*" came out of its hiding, assuming the position on the embankment again and commenced fire with all the barrels. Soon, however, the fire of the cannons had to be halted, as they fired straight ahead and the fuses set to immediate detonation caused premature explosions in the tree tops – shell fragments injured own troops. On the other hand, the howitzers performed their task flawlessly and turned out to be quite effective anti-tank weapons. Most of the German tanks were *Pz.Kpfw. I* and *II* vehicles, small and light, so no direct hits were even necessary – the nearby howitzer blasts threw the tanks into the air and knocked them over. The Germans could not withstand the murderous fire, leaving wrecked tanks and their dead in the field. After the enemy had withdrawn, the train was ordered to move to Działoszyn; from there it began to patrol the Działoszyn – Miedzno section of the line. Around 15:00 hours at the Miedzno station, Captain Malinowski was ordered by radio to advance towards the area of Mokra III village, where – as was suspected – German armour was attempting a breakthrough. German aircraft detected the movement of "*Śmiały*" and attacked it. A flight of six planes dropped a total of 15 bombs from an altitude of approximately 200 to 300 m. None of them hit the train, although their explosions shook the carriages

Armoured locomotive Ti3-9 in German service at Tarnopol station (coupled with "Marszałek" artillery wagon). Probably in 1941.

Artillery wagon of "Śmiały" in German hands. To the far right, a fragment of "Marszałek" artillery wagon.

roughly and number of fragments pierced the armour.

The P.P. 53 armoured train reached the bridge over the Liswarta River without any major damage. As the train made a short stop by the river, German tanks passed through Miedzno station to the east. About 15:30 hours the train commander received an order calling him to return to the vast fields of the village of Mokra III. Several minutes earlier, the Germans began preparations for their most powerful assault of the day, engaging over a hundred tanks an equivalent of an entire armoured brigade. The train set off again travelling slowly, in anticipation of an encounter with the enemy. Still, contact with a German armoured – motorised column at a forest edge near the crossing of the track with the Rębielice – Izbiska road was quite unexpected. It was a surprise for both sides – since the Germans were busy with refuelling, among other things. The crew of P.P. 53 opened heavy fire on German vehicles on both sides of the track. The troopers of the trains' assault platoon were also brought into combat. At the most heated moment, P.P. 52 "Piłsudczyk" appeared, coming from the neighbouring sector of the 30. Dywizja Piechoty (30th Division). The fighting lasted about 30 minutes, the train was slowly moving back and forth along the enemy lines. When the fighting was over, there were several dozen destroyed vehicles left in the clearing. After the moment of surprise, the crews of the tanks farther from the crossing tamed their pannic, and some guns accompanying the German infantry took up positions and opened fire. "Śmiały", shielded by the fire of "Piłsudczyk", had to withdraw, but the German attack collapsed completely and the remaining tanks retreated in disarray. Both trains departed towards Działoszyn.

The German air force tried to intervene during the action, but the howitzers firing at their highest elevation with shrapnel rounds managed to effectively weaken the aviators' enthusiasm. Nonetheless, they dropped bombs on the track, cutting off "Piłsudczyk" on its way back to Siemkowice. The crews of both trains participated in the repair of the tracks.

The trains arrived at Siemkowice at dawn on 2 September. "Śmiały" was placed at the disposal of the 30. Dywizja Piechoty, and was ordered to move to the Siemkowice – Częstochowa line. The train came across a column of tanks coming from the direction of Kłobuck which it shelled effectively, and at Cykarzewo it again opened fire on German motor transport and tanks.

In the evening of 2 September, the armoured train and its echelon was dispatched to the Łask station, and on 3 September to Łódź. There, P.P. 53 placed at the disposal of the Armia "Prusy" was ordered to travel to Koluszki. Koluszki railway junction was plagued by air raids, so the crew had to do a lot of track clearing. On 4 September the P.P. 55 also arrived in Koluszki. The next day, German aircraft attacked the station several times. The armoured trains did not suffer any damage, but the sidings on which the administrative supply trains stood were completely demolished and it was not possible to move one of the trains out. From then on, the administrative section of "Bartosz Głowacki" also had to serve "Śmiały".

On 6 September, both trains were one after the other patrolling the line to Skierniewice, and in the evening they halted in Skierniewice.

On 7 September "Śmiały" managed to survive another air raid without losses – but the tracks were seriously damaged and a reconnaissance to Łowicz could not be carried out.

Cropped and enlarged fragment of photographs depicting "Śmiały" artillery wagons.

Movement became possible on the next day, 8 September. Both trains, covering each other, were patrolling the Skierniewice – Żyrardów line, and in the evening – together with the administrative section of the "Głowacki" – they headed for Warsaw. Having been assigned to the *Armia "Modlin"*, they were ordered to travel to Mińsk Mazowiecki. The trains did not attempt travel through Warsaw, but instead – via Warszwa – Gdańska station – they went to Legionowo and Zegrze, and from there, taking the seldom used Zegrze-Tłuszcz line, to Mińsk Mazowiecki. The route from Mińsk to Siedlce was congested with transport trains, therefore movement was seriously hindered.

In Siedlce it was learned that the enemy was approaching the town, so the trains had to leave in a hurry, more so because concentration of the Polish troops was supposed to take place in Łuków.

Both trains, following each other, arrived in Łuków on 11 September. There was no concentration of troops whatsoever; insead the trains were subjected to another enemy air raid. Any further travel was only possible after the tracks were repaired. The raid brought suspicions that someone had been directing the aircraft – and indeed, the patrols captured two two-man enemy teams, armed and equipped with radios.

On 12 September, after the tracks had been repaired and the wreckage removed, the trains set off on the line leading to Brześć. In Międzyrzecze the Chief-of-Staff of the *33. Dywizja Piechoty* (33rd Division) ordered further travel to the Brześć Fortress. On 13 September the trains arrived in Brześć.

On the following day, P.P. 53 was ordered to reconnoitre in the direction of Wysokie – at the little station of Skoki, the train supported the infantry of the KOP (*Korpus Ochrony Pogranicza* – Border

Cropped and enlarged view of armoured train "Śmiały".

Protection Corps). Return to the Fortress proved impossible, as the Germans were already in Brześć – the only open route was the track to Kowel. The crews managed to replenish the coal supply and take it the water, and on 15 September in the evening the trains reached Kowel. The relative calm allowed for maintenance of the steam engine, including flushing of the boiler.

On 16 September, the trains were ordered to depart from Kowel to Lwów. The shortest route, through Włodzimierz, was jammed with transports, so the trains took a detour through Kiwerce.

On 17 September, P.P. 53 and P.P. 55 reached Kiwerce station – here the news arrived of the attack by the Soviets. A decision was made to break through to Lwów – after track repairs and clearing of wreckage, both trains moved past Łuck.

On 18 September, forward German units were already scouting around Lwów – after a short firefight, both trains reached Lwów – Podzamcze station on the eastern side of the city. On the same day, "Śmiały" was relocated to Lwów – Łyczaków station to support the defence. The next day P.P. 53 supported the counterattack on Zboiska with its artillery, then moved to-

Artillery wagon of "Śmiały" in German service.

wards Sapieżanka, harassing the German infantry approaching from the east. In the evening the train came to Podzamcze, from where it opened fire on German positions near Zamarstynów, and at night it returned to the Lwów – Łyczaków station.

On 20 September, it once again supported renewed counterattack on Zboiska, which this time was successful.

On 21 September, the fire of German artillery ceased, the Germans began to withdraw troops from Lwów, and the next day Lwów surrendered. Red Army troops entered the city.

Armoured train "Śmiały" was taken over by the Red Army. After inspection at Lwów, it was commissioned by the *NKVD* forces as the *Bronepoyezd* of the 75th Regiment of the 10th *NKVD* Division. The emblems displaying the White Eagle were torn off, but that was basically the extent of the changes. The steam locomotive was assigned as *Zheleznodorozhony Bronirowanny Obyekt nomer 103* (Armoured Railway Object Number 103 – *ZhBO-103*), wagon 699020 – *ZhBO-104*, wagon 699021 – *ZhBO-105*. The assault wagon was not included in the train.

It remained in Lwów with the new designation *ZhBO-106*. For unknown reason, the Soviets removed the lower part of the armour from it, dismantled the antenna masts (hence the conclusion that they also removed the wireless set), and painted the number 840078 with a stencil on the undercarriage which was exposed after the armour belt protecting it had been disassembled.

The train was captured by the Germans on 7 July 1941. Russian sources mention its heroic battle with enemy tanks and fighting to the last round, after

which it was blown up, but this is very unlikely, since by December 1941 the rolling stock was included in the *Kampfzug A*. Over time the composition was modified – the locomotive was replaced, other wagons were added. The train was eventually renumbered *Panzerzug 10* and finally lost in Kowel in March 1944. One artillery wagon survived, it was towed to what was the German base in Rembertów, but never returned to service.

Artillery wagon of "Śmiały" *in German service (during refitting prior to forming* Kampfzug A*).*

Armoured Train P.P. 54
(P.P. 6 "Groźny")

Armoured Train No. 54 was mobilised during the so-called silent mobilisation on 2 May 1939. It was the former Armoured Train No. 6 "Groźny". Captain Jan Rybczyński (mobilisation officer of the 2. *Dywizjon*) was appointed its commanding officer; his deputy was Captain Józef Kulesza.

P.P. 54 "Groźny" at the Swoszowice station surrounded by German troops in 1939.

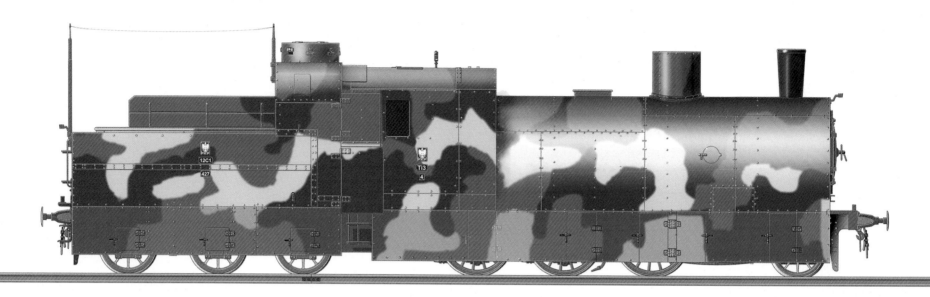

A profile of "Groźny" Ti3-4 armoured locomotive.

Armoured train "Groźny" at Swoszowice.

Locomotive

The locomotive was *Ti3* Number 4 with tender *12C1* Number 427. Produced by Hanomag in 1904, German number 4023 Danzig (factory number 4116). The turret on the tender in the early 1930's was changed to a cylindrical one with a larger diameter.

Armoured locomotive of "Groźny" at the Swoszowice siding.

The turret with the wz.02/26 cannon of the artillery wagon 460012.

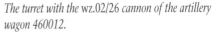

A profile of the 460012 artillery wagon.

Artillery wagons

The front wagon had the number 450025. It belonged to the so-called "*Izhorski*" type – with two turrets of the "*Sormovo*" type, same as the turrets of the "*Marszałek*", armed with 75 mm *wz. 02/26* cannons. The wagon was built on the chassis of a large four-axle American Drop Bottom Gondola type coal railcar. The rear artillery wagon was numbered 450012. It is also referred to as the "*Izhorski*" type. An American coal railcar was also used in its construction, but it had cylindrical turrets with a 100 mm howitzer in one and a 75 mm cannon in the other.

Four photographs depicting "Groźny" at Biadoliny station.

Next page:
Artillery wagon 460012 seen from the side of the howitzer turret. On the right, a fragment of the assault wagon. Photograph taken at Swoszowice station.

A profile of the 460025 artillery wagon.

Preceding page:
Artillery wagon 460025 and the tender of the Ti3-4 locomotive. It may be noticed that the flat railcar is a commercial Pdks version.

To the right:
Artillery wagon 460025 Swoszowice station.

Below:
Two partial views of the 460025 artillery wagon and the 12C1-427 coal tender.

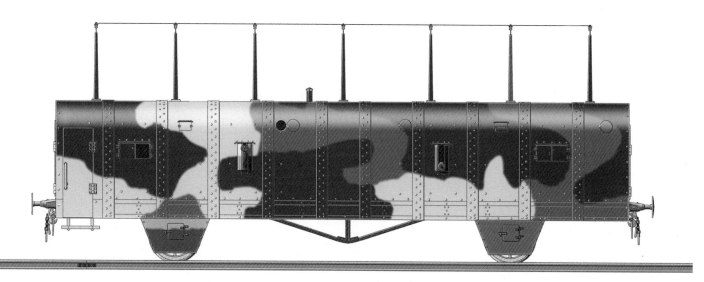

A profile of the 631550 assault wagon.

Assault wagon

The assault wagon had the number 631550 and was converted from a single-turret artillery wagon on a chassis of an Austrian *Jk* series flat railcar with a brakeman's cab. Two similar – but not identical wagons were in service during 1920's. One of them was an artillery wagon assigned to P.P. 15 *"Paderewski"* in 1920 – the documentation is uncertain, but some details in the photographs point to this particular one. The conversion was quite extensive as the section of the roof underneath the dismantled turret had to be replaced. As part of the adaptation typical heavy machine gun mounts were installed, so were the posts for the aerial antennae. An enclosed radio compartment was constructed inside the armoured casemate.

Combat flat railcars

Standard flat railcars of the *Pdks* series with a loading length of 13 m, supplied by *P.K.P.* They were an ex-German *C143* flat railcars or Polish production *C-VIII* series, identical to them. An information exists that the train had three, not two, combat flat railcars, but this cannot be verified.

The photograph depicts the front of the "Piłsudczyk" locomotive, two artillery and one assault wagons of "Groźny" followed by the artillery and assault wagons of "Piłsudczyk" after transfer to a siding at Krakow railway station.

Draisine platoon

Standard two sets of draisines *TK-R-TK*. Four *TKS* type tankettes and two *Renault FT* tanks, supplemented by a spare *TKS* tankette – it is not known whether with a rail guide or not.

Administrative Supply Train Section

A civilian "black" steam locomotive and wagons delivered by the *DOKP Kraków*. Most likely the composition was in line with the regulations. A lorry and motorcycles were carried on the section's flat railcars.

Both of the artillery wagons and the assault wagon of "Groźny" in Cracow. Below: Armoured train P.P. 54 "Groźny" at unidentified location – possibly Swoszowice.

Following two pages: The remnants of two TK-R-TK draisine sets at the Swoszowice station.

Previous page:
A situation not yet explained – the R-TK draisine arrangement was hit and demolished by a Pdks flat railcar; whether it was an accident or an intentional sabotage remains unknown.
This page:
Three images of the damaged draisine equipment loaded on flat railcars for transport.

Totally destroyed tankette in front of the flat railcar loaded with the Renault FT tank on the transporter and a TK rail guide

"Grоźny" in September 1939

In June, July and August, the train crew was being intensively trained. From 26 August, the train was in a siding at Krzeszowice. It was assigned to the *Grupa Operacyjna "Śląsk"* (Operational Group "Silesia") and the area of Upper Silesia was its future battlefield.

On the day of the outbreak of the war, in the morning of 1 September, the armoured train along with the administrative supply echelon left for Mikołów. In Mikołów it turned out that the actions of German saboteurs could threaten the administrative train, so it was sent to the Ligota station near Katowice. The first German bombs fell on the train in Mikołów, but to no effect. The combat section advanced through Mysłowice to Tychy.

From Tychy, *"Grоźny"* set off on a reconnaissance in the direction of Orzesze, where it successfully fired on advancing German infantry. Before noon that day, having collected the wounded of the "Mikołów Redoubt", it went back to Tychy. Then it patrolled the Tychy – Kobiór line, where German troops began to break through. In the evening, the train was subordinated to the commander of the 23. *Dywizja Piechoty* (23rd Division), with the task of supporting it in the area of the village of Wyry, west of Tychy. The train came under attack by bombers.

On 2 September, P.P. 54 supported the battalion of the 73. *Pułk Piechoty* (73rd Infantry Regiment) covering Tychy with its gunfire. Then, it took an active part in the

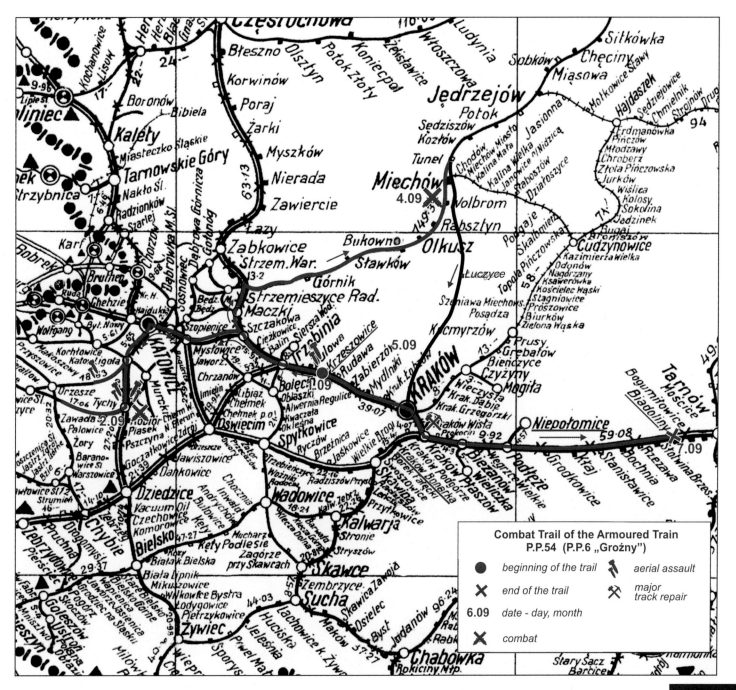

Combat Trail of the Armoured Train P.P.54 (P.P.6 „Grоźny")

- ● beginning of the trail
- ✗ end of the trail
- **6.09** date - day, month
- ✗ combat
- ⚒ aerial assault
- ⚒ major track repair

Polish counterattack in the Wyry region, cooperating directly with the infantry. The Polish infantry attacked southwards, on the west side of the Tychy – Kobiór railway line. The train was advancing alongside the infantry, inflicting heavy losses on German troops. After the Germans were forced out of the woods near Wyry, the train departed for Tychy, evacuating the wounded soldiers, and then returned to action in the afternoon. An attempt to use the assault platoon at the intersection with the road to Żwaków around 14:00 hours failed under the fire of enemy mortars and machine guns. The train pulled back, only to return a short time later, firing with all barrels. Until the evening the train harassed the enemy with rapid sorties, despite air attacks (several bombs fell right next to the train, but they did not explode, and in another raid, bombs were dropped along the track) and artillery fire. After 16:00 hours P.P. 54 arrived at Tychy station with a new load of wounded collected from the battlefield.

Captain Rybczyński took a tankette to assess the situation out in the field several times. His last reconnaissance, around 18:00 hours ended tragically – Captain Rybczyński walked away from the tankette and never came back. Command was taken over by his deputy Captain Józef Kulesza. The train was withdrawn to Mysłowice via Katowice.

The armament of armoured train "Groźny" – the howitzer turret of artillery wagon 460012 and a close-up of the cannon on the 460025 wagon.

On 3 September, P.P. 54 performed one more sortie towards Tychy and Wyry, shooting at the approaching Germans, and then moved through Jaworzno, to the Szczakowa station. Later, it was ordered to travel to the Olkusz – Wolbrom line, while the administrative train was sent to Krzeszowice.

On 4 September, the administrative section was ordered to travel to Cracow, while the combat section reached the Cracow – Kielce main line. A successful exchange of fire with a German motorised unit took place near the Tunel station.

During the night of 4/5 September, P.P. 54 travelled to Cracow. Darkness, fog or probably extreme fatigue made the train run over its own set of draisines. Lieutenant Bogdan Wilkoszewski died; the wrecks of the rail guide and tankette had to be pushed off the track.

In Cracow, the crew managed to partially replenish supplies and both the armoured and administrative trains left Cracow on the night of 5/6 September, heading for Cracow – Płaszów station. The leading team of draisines discovered damage to the track and a repair was needed.

On 7 September, P.P. 54 arrived at the Biadoliny station. It turned out, however, that the bridge over the Dunajec River at Bogumiłowice was blown up (there was a pile of twisted steel with no chance for repair; before it was blown up, empty wagons had been left on the bridge to increase the destruction effect) so it was no longer possible to travel further to Tarnów. In the rear of the train the bridge in Podłęże was blown up by engineers. When German patrols started to approach the area, Captain Kulesza gave orders to set explosive charges in the locomotive, remove gun breeches, take the machine guns and abandon the train. Some of the soldiers joined the P.P. 51 in Rozwadów. A second group marched towards Lwów, but after the invasion of the Soviets, turned back to Warsaw and on their way there joined *Grupa Operacyjna "Polesie"*.

The rolling stock captured by the Germans was later used in armoured trains. *Panzerzug 21* had artillery wagon number 460012 (with a 100 mm howitzer and a 75 mm cannon) and an assault wagon from "*Groźny*". A composition of *Pz.21* included second artillery wagon from "*Piłsudczyk*", and a third, small, single-turret wagon from the exercise train. The locomotive *Ti3-13* came from "*Piłsudczyk*", and was assigned German number 54654. With time, the locomotive and composition of *Pz.21* were changed, but the core components remained the same. The train was used in combat on the Eastern Front and on 30 October 1944 it was captured by the Soviet troops in Mazeikiai in Lithuania.

An artillery wagon of "Groźny" pressed in German service as part of the Pz.22. The sides of the gun turrets were slightly modified – the top edges were bevelled to fit within the Western European train clearance gauge.

Panzerzug 22 received a wagon with two 75 mm cannons from *"Groźny"* (Polish number 460025), an assault wagon from *"Piłsudczyk"* and a single-turret wagon from the exercise train. The *Ti3-4* locomotive from the *"Groźny"* was assigned to the train with number 54651. The train, partially modified, served mainly in France, and at the end of the war it was transferred to the Eastern Front. *Panzerzug 22* was destroyed on 11 February 1945 in Szprotawa.

A close-up of the Panzerzug 22 artillery wagon – a side taper of the turret's armour is well visible.

Panzerzug 21 – artillery wagon from "Groźny", followed by a single turret reserve Exercise Train artillery wagon, and two assault wagons of Polish provenance.

Armoured Train P.P. 55
(P.P. 10 "Bartosz Głowacki")

The P.P. 10 "*Bartosz Głowacki*" was mobilised as the Armoured Train No. 55. It was commanded by Captain Andrzej Podgórski (formerly commander of the armoured draisine company), his second-in-command was Lieutenant Edward Massalski.

On the right, an artillery wagon of "Bartosz Głowacki" before final modifications. The photograph was taken at the Grzegórzki training ground in 1930. In the foreground, the pioneers of the 1st Battalion of Railway Bridges are erecting a provisional overpass. Some additional armoured wagons are visible on the siding in the background. Some modifications were carried out at the 2nd Armoured Group's workshop; the major ones were performed by Krakow Armoury or railway repair shops in Krakow and Nowy Sącz.

A profile of Ti3-10 locomotive.

A side view of Ti3-10 as ZhBO-020.

Locomotive

A typical armoured *Ti3* number 10, produced by the BMAG factory in 1904. German number 4015 Posen (factory number 3372). Tender *12C1* number 478. The command post on the tender of this locomotive had a cylindrical observation turret with eight observation slits.

Artillery wagons

Polish construction, "warsaw" type, two-axle, single turret, with 75 mm cannons *wz. 02/26*. They had numbers 630728 and 630729 (their previous numbers were 02005 and 02029). The design of this type of wagon was developed at the beginning of 1920 in the Warsaw branch of the *Kierownictwo Budowy Pociągów Pancernych* (Armoured Train Construction Directorate).

The armour was installed on typical Tsarist standard flat railcars with a load capacity of 1,000 poods. This armour had a characteristic semi-barrel shape. Artillery wagons of the "warsaw" type, which were part of the P.P. 55 train, were initially armed with the 3-inch Lender cannons (76.2 mm *wz. 02* gun designed for anti-aircraft fire), and finally with *wz. 02/26* cannons – preserving the original mountings of the Lender system. The heavy machine gun firing ports, at first just ordinary rectangular openings with sliding screens, were replaced in the 1930's with typical cylindrical mounts. The heavy

Artillery wagon of "Bartosz Głowacki", *number 630728 around 1935.*

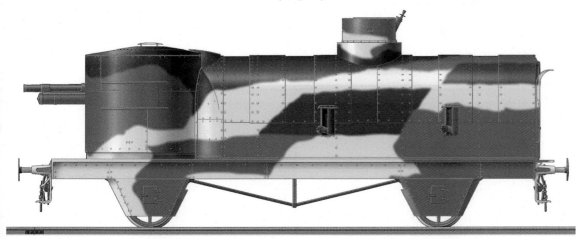

A profile of artillery wagon 630728.

Artillery wagon of "Bartosz Głowacki", *number 630728 as Soviet ZhBO-021.*

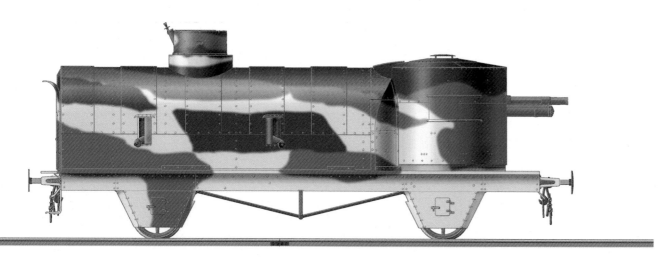

A profile of artillery wagon 630729.

machine gun turrets atop the roof were replaced with standardized anti-aircraft turrets. The intention was to strengthen the P.P. 55 composition with a howitzer wagon (number 630727, earlier 02006; until the mid-1930s it remained at the *Pole Ćwiczeń* – Training Field – in Cracow, still armed with an Austrian 8 cm cannon), but in the end did not take place, and the wagon – at the time rearmed with a howitzer – found itself in the Exercise Train of the Reserve Detachment.

Artillery wagon of "Bartosz Głowacki", number 630729 as Soviet ZhBO-022.

Assault wagon

The wagon had the number 630726 and, just like the artillery wagons of the train, it was of the "warsaw" type. At first, it was one of the four artillery wagons of this type with an Austrian 8 cm cannon (construction details visible in the photographs support this). In the 1930's extensive alterations were made – the turret was removed and the resulting gap was filled by extending the half-barrel profiled casemate armour. Cylindrical heavy machine gun mounts were installed, the heavy machine gun turret was removed from the roof, and new upright masts were fitted with antenna cables stretched between them. Double-panel doors in the side walls were fitted (shifted in relation to each other on the left and right side of the wagon). A wireless radio set compartment was created inside. The under-frame was covered with an additional armour belt, and the axle grease-boxes of the wheels were covered by trapezoidal armoured plates with inspection doors.

A profile of assault wagon 630726.

Assault wagon of "Bartosz Głowacki", number 630726 around 1935.

Assault wagon of "Bartosz Głowacki" captured by the Germans from the Soviets.

Below, left:
"Bartosz Głowacki" wagon among other captured armoured wagons serving with the Red Army.

Below:
Modified assault wagon of "Bartosz Głowacki" as part of German armoured train Panzerzug 10.

Combat flat railcars

Standard flat railcars of the *Pdks* series with a loading length of 13 m, were supplied by *P.K.P.* These were either ex-German *C143* platforms or identical Polish *C-VIII* series. At around 11 September, a 40 mm anti-aircraft gun found in Łuków was placed on one of them.

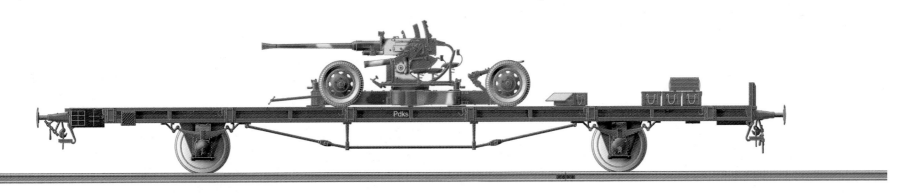

A profile of flat Pdks railcar with 40 mm antiaircraft cannon.

An R tank transporter, TK rail guide and a Renault FT tank form "Bartosz Głowacki" abandoned at Żabinka.

A fragment of TK rail guide and a Renault FT tank form "Bartosz Głowacki".

Draisine platoon

Standard – two *R* draisines with *Renault FT* tanks, four *TK* draisines with *TKS* tankettes. It is not known whether the train had a fifth, spare, draisine.

Administrative Supply Train Section

A civilian steam locomotive and wagons delivered by the *DOKP Kraków*. Most likely, the composition was in line with the regulations. On the train's flat railcars, there was a 2-ton lorry (we do not know what type), a *Polski Fiat 508* with van body and two *Sokół 1000* motorcycles.

"Bartosz Głowacki" in September 1939

On 27 August 1939, the train left Cracow – Bonarka armoured train depot with a route planned to Tłuszcz, near Warsaw.

1 September passed peacefully, but the very next day German planes appeared over Tłuszcz, strafing the station and the standing transport trains. Luckily, the armoured train did not suffer any damage. On the same day, it was decided the train would go to Skierniewice (it was assigned to the *Armia "Prusy"*).

On 4 September, P.P. 55 was moved to Koluszki. In Koluszki it met with the P.P. 53 ("*Śmiały*"), also directed there. Fol-

A Renault tank at Żabinka. All hatches are open and the trench crossing tail is partially disconnected.

lowing day, on 5 September, the Koluszki railway junction was attacked several times by aircraft – neither train suffered, but the damage was so extensive that despite the efforts of railwaymen and trains' crews, the tracks were not cleared for the P.P. 55 to move out towards Piotrków, into action.

On 6 September, the train patrolled the Koluszki – Skierniewice line, and on 7 September it was halted in Skierniewice. A heavy air raid paralysed the station and prevented the intended patrol of the line to Łowicz.

On 8 September, the train reconnoitred the Skierniewice – Żyrardów route and towards the end of the day was ordered to withdraw to Warsaw.

On 10 September, this time subordinate to the *Armia "Modlin"*, *"Bartosz Głowacki"* was ordered to move to Siedlce. It travelled via Jabłonna, Tłuszcz and Mińsk Mazowiecki. There was a huge congestion in the vicinity of Siedlce – the train crew (with the aid administrative echelon's and the P.P. 53's crew, as both trains travelled together at the time) had to clear off the wreckage, repair the track and even build short detours. In Siedlce it turned out that German troops were already approaching the town, so the train left Siedlce and headed for Łuków, since a concentration of troops was expected there. On 11 September (or possibly on the 12) a 40 mm anti-aircraft gun was found abandoned at the Łuków station – it was mounted on the combat flat car, and turned out to be very useful in future combat. On 12 September, after the tracks had been repaired, the trains travelled through Międzyrzecze, where an order was received to continue to Brześć. Both trains arrived at the Fortress on 13 September.

On 14 September, the command of the Brześć Fortress sent the P.P. 55 for reconnaissance to Żabinka, to the junction of the railway lines to Kobryń (single track line to Łuniniec), and the double track line to Baranowicze. In Żabinka, all the tankettes and both *Renault FT* tanks (one *FT* tank remained near the track for unknown reasons) moved off their rail transporters and went for a field reconnaissance. They were forced to take up an unequal engagement with German armoured cars which unfortunately they lost, but the crews managed to return to the train. Meanwhile, a column of German tanks and motorcycle troops approached on the road from Kamieniec Litewski. Train Number 55, standing at the road crossing, forced the Germans to turn back, destroying several vehicles with gun fire. A group of tanks made an

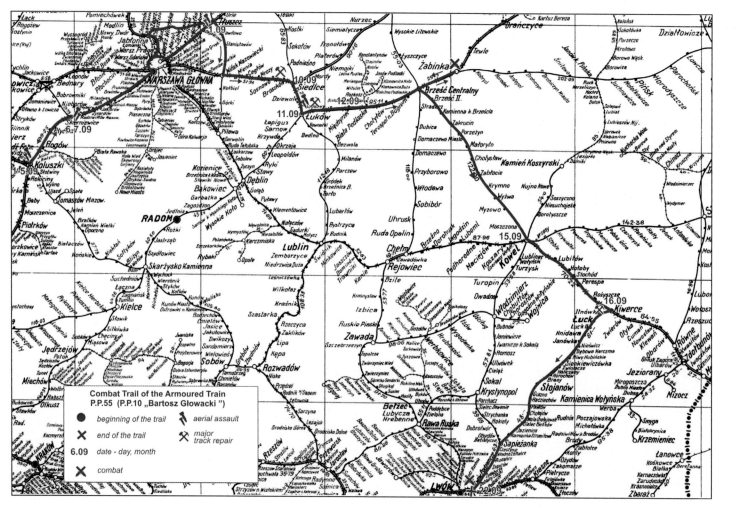

Combat route of armoured train "Bartosz Głowacki".

A Renault *tank*, TK *rail guide and some uninvited visitors.*

Above:
The Renault *tank from "Bartosz Głowacki" generated considerable interest.*

The Renault *tank drove off the transporter, but remained by the tracks for unknown reasons. The arrangement of the broken track indicates that the tank was in reverse gear when the failure took place. The damage to one of the links suggests that a nearby explosion of some sort could have had occurred. There are numerous photographs of this scene which leads to a belief that the tank remained in place for a considerably long time after it was abandoned.*

The TKS *tankette from* "Bartosz Głowacki" *at the roadside near Żabinka.*

German soldiers by the TKS tankette from "Bartosz Głowacki".

attempt to outflank the train, but the train's guns successfully stopped them. A short while later the train was shelled by a German artillery. After about 45 minutes of artillery duelling, P.P. 55 withdrew to Brześć, but the city was already partially occupied by the Germans – the train was ordered to withdraw via the only available route to Kowel (P.P. 53 also set off to Kowel).

"*Bartosz Głowacki*" arrived in Kowel on 15 September; a much needed respite was used to carry out some maintenance tasks – it was high time to flush the steam locomotive's boiler. Other equipment was inspected and material supplies were replenished.

On 17 September, the P.P. 55 and P.P. 53 arrived at the Kiwerce station – once there, the crews learned the news of the Soviet attack. A decision was made to break through to Lwów. After the tracks were repaired and the wreckage removed, both trains moved via Łuck. There were already some German forces scouting the vicinity of Lwów – after a brief firefight, both trains reached the Lwów – Podzamcze station on the eastern side of the city.

On 18 September, the trains alternately patrolled the close vicinity of the station, and on 19 September P.P. 55 supported the counterattack of Polish infantry on Hołosko (north of Lwów). The train was shelled by German artillery, which scored several indirect hits – "*Bartosz Głowacki*", losing steam from the pierced boiler, returned to Podzamcze (according to one report it was shunted away by a civilian steam locomotive). The repair took all night, but the next day the train was again fit for combat and resumed patrol duties.

On 22 September, Lwów surrendered to the Soviet troops entering the city, in accordance to the agreement outlining the occupation zones between the USSR and Germany. The train crew laid down their arms around 11:00 hours.

The Soviet military re-commissioned "*Bartosz Głowacki*" to serve as the *Bronepoyezd* (armoured train) of the 58th *NKVD* Regiment. Initially, it was used around Lwów. It is not known whether the train also included the assault wagon – probably not (Soviet regulations did not call for an infantry / assault / machine gun wagon to be included in an armoured train assembly). The train was destroyed or abandoned during the retreat of the Soviet troops in June 1941.

The assault wagon of the P.P. 55 was captured by the Germans in 1941 in Lwów and was used from then until 1944 in the German armoured train *Panzerzug 10*. The Germans also captured the *Ti3-10* locomotive from the Soviets. It is listed, with the German number 54657, in the service of the *Deutsche Reichsbahn* – as an un-armoured locomotive.

TKS *tankette from* "Bartosz Głowacki" *abandoned by the road was rising continues interest of* Wehrmacht *troops passing by.*

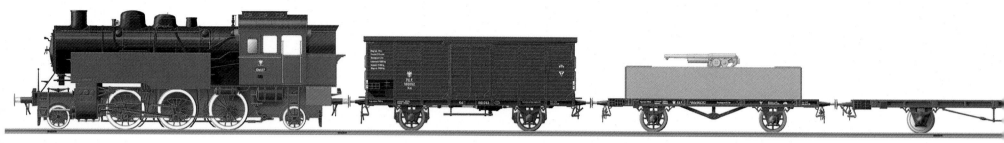

ANNEX

Next page:
It is impossible to establish the assignment of this
Renault *tank on a rail transporter, nor the location at*
which the photograph was taken. It is most likely the
equipment of the 1. Dywizjon Pociągów Pancernych
(1ˢᵗ Armoured Trains Group).

Unidentified Draisines

There is no difficulty with the recognition of the Polish armoured trains photographed by the German troops in September of 1939. The draizines, on the other hand, are a problem since many were abandoned or destroyed some distance away from their respective combat trains. The surrounding terrain captured in an image almost never provides a clue as to the actual location – usually there are no characteristic features. To make matters worse, even if a photograph from the era has a caption, there is no certainty – it is a common occurrence that the descriptions are inaccurate.

Tatra draisine taken over and pressed in service by the Germans. To the right, Panzerzug 1. The draisine retains Polish camouflage painting. It could have come from the 1. Dywizjon, but it is not impossible that it was assigned to the Armoured Group in Cracow.

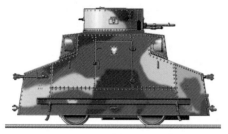

Tatra draisine from the 1. Dywizjon Pociągów Pancernych. It was not possible to establish if it left for the front with the P.P. 13 or P.P. 15.

The R rail transporter coupled with an empty TK rail guide. The time and place unknown – the terrain does not provide any clues.

Some TK and R equipment loaded on Flat railcars prior to shipment to the scrap yard. The damaged draisines were usually pushed off the tracks so there is no indication of their prior assignments.

Below:
Two photographs of the R draisine, the same one as on page 327. The first image taken at the original location, the second elsewhere. The surroundings do not offer any hints as to the location.

IMPROVISED TRAINS

The First LOW Train

In 1939 the *LOW* – *Lądowa Obrona Wybrzeża* (Coastal Land Defence) had no armoured equipment available. Towards the end of August a combat train was constructed using commercial railway rolling stock. It was referred to as an improvised train nr. I. In fact, the train consisted of two nearly identical sets of railcars (during the course of the September Campaign they operated independently). The train was commissioned on 26 August.

The artillery wagons were constructed on the basses of flat railcars series *Pdkłz* originally equipped with lumber cradles and side stanchions. The floor was reinforced with a layer of hardwood. The front and rear walls were also constructed of thick hardwood boards. The sides were protected with a twin layer of sheet metal affixed to the shortened stanchions. Steel ledge extended all the way across the length covering the gap between the side plates. It is possible that the space between the sheet metal plates was filled with sand or concrete.

The 75 mm cannons on naval mounts were placed in the centre of the wagon.

The combat crew was transported in a typical covered goods wagon *Kd*. According to the relations form the era, sand bags were stacked inside to provide protection. Two 15 ton capacity flat *Pdks* wagons complemented the train.

Typical Polish timber flat railcar with rotating cradle.

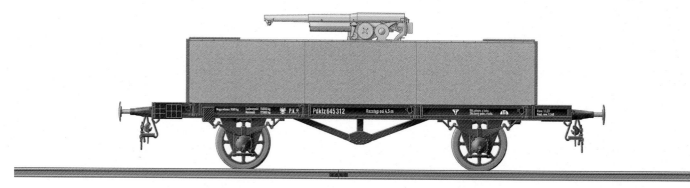

The artillery wagon with a 75 mm naval cannon used in Kartuzy. The second wagon was nearly identical.

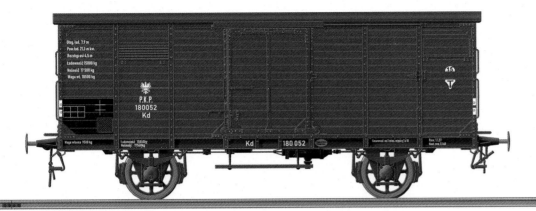

Covered wagon of the Kd series with air break system – such wagons were adopted for LOW improvised combat trains.

Two tank locomotives of Polish construction – *OKl27* type were assigned to provide motive power (*DOKP Toruń* [National Railways Regional Authority] had 28 *OKl27* locomotives – 17 stationed in Gdańsk and 11 in Gdynia). The designation translated as follows: *O – osobowy* (passenger), *K – kusy* (tank w/o tender), *l – oOOOo* (axle arrangement), *27 – rok* (year of introduction).

On 1 September 1939 the train was divided, one section patrolled the track between Kartuzy – Somonino, while the other in the area of Stara Piła. In the following few days the trains patroled the area in the vicinity of Somonin and Żukowo.

The connection to Gdynia was breached by the Germans on 4 September so the train was cut off and lost its operational ability.

The Second LOW Train

This improvised train was deployed for only two days 3 and 4 of September. Two covered goods wagons – protected by crates filled with sand, pulled by a locomotive clad in steel plates, carried an assault platoon armed with machine guns. On 4 September the train engaged the enemy near Wielki Kack in support of Polish counter attack towards Osowa and Wysoka.

Left, and next page:
The equipment of the First combat train of the LOW stored by the Germans at the Kartuzy station.

Armoured Train
"Smok Kaszubski"

On 7 September the Naval Dockyard at Gdynia completed an armoured train called "*Smok Kaszubski*" ("Kashubian Dragon"). An *OKl27* locomotive, two covered goods wagons and two open coal wagons were provided with armoured plates. Two or four flat railcars were added. The armament consisted of one 47 mm *Hotchkiss* cannon – the accounts citing the 40 mm *Bofors* guns are not probable. The mentions of a 40 mm *Vickers* gun, removed from the torpedo boat "*Mazur*" sunk few days prior, are also inaccurate.

On 8 September, the train exchanged fire with German patrols and armoured cars at Wejherowo. On 9 September the train sustained damage in the artillery duel with German batteries and withdrew to Reda, and than to Rumia. In the following days, 10 and 11 September, the train provided artillery support for Polish troops defending Rumia and Zagórze. The day after, the train defended Kępa Oksywska. In the course of action German air attack damaged the train completely destroying one of the wagons. After withdrawal to Gdynia, the repairs were carried out and on 14 September combat readiness was restored but the train remained in the workshop as Polish troops abandoned the town to concentrate or the defence of Oksywie.

A view of the artillery wagon with naval 75 mm cannon from Kartuzy. The second wagon, seen in the background, was almost identical.

The locomotive Okl27-8 – this type of locomotive was used to operate the improvised trains of LOW coastal defence.

A profiles of the freight – passenger tank locomotive series Okl27, right and left side. Difference in a paint scheme is noteworthy.

Palmiry – Warsaw Train

Around 12 September an improvised combat train was assembled to provide transport and protect the vital railroad line connecting Warszawa with the main ammunition depot in Palmiry. It was deemed necessary in view of the German scout units making raids toward the outposts of Warszawa defences. The train was arranged at the *Warszawa-Gdańska* station using the typical *Kd* covered goods wagons, intended for ammunition transport, and some flat railcars carrying the guns. The armament consisted of a 75 mm field gun, two 37 mm anti tank guns and two heavy machine guns manned by three officers and approximately 60 soldiers. The train made the round trip to Palmiry twice, without any incidents. The activities were suspended when the track, previously only exposed to German air attacks, came in range of advancing enemy heavy artillery. At that point it was beyond the ability of the railroad personnel and the supporting army pioneer units stationed at Warszawa-Gdańska to continue with track repairs.

Vilnius Train

During the defensive battles with the soviet Red Army attacking from the east, an improvised armoured train was formed. On 18 September it was dispatched to protect the railroad line Wilno – Lida. The train was damaged and, in result, abandoned after the engagement with soviet tanks – the crew withdrew to Wilno (Vilnius).

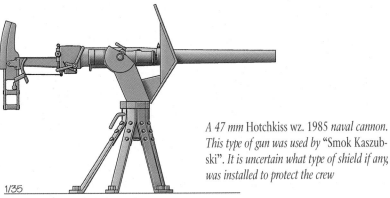

A 47 mm Hotchkiss wz. 1985 naval cannon. This type of gun was used by "Smok Kaszubski". It is uncertain what type of shield if any, was installed to protect the crew

1/35

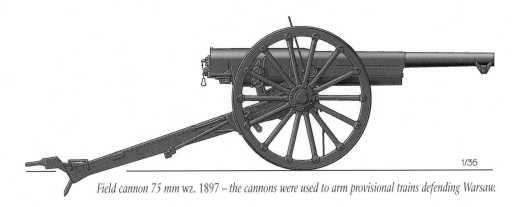

1/35

Field cannon 75 mm wz. 1897 – the cannons were used to arm provisional trains defending Warsaw.

No. 1 and No. 2 Warsaw Defence Trains

On 20 September the Warsaw Defence Command (*Dowództwo Obrony Warszawy*) put forth a request to form two improvised combat trains, designated No. 1 and No. 2. The first train, completed on 22 September, had two 75 mm cannons and two heavy machine guns placed on provisionally armoured flat railcars. It was assigned to the "*Warszawa-Zachód*" ("Warsaw – West") defence sector. The second improvised train created on 23 September, was assigned directly to the *Dowództwo Obrony Warszawy*. It was armed with two 75 mm cannons, a 37 mm anti-tank gun and machine guns. The appearance and combat history of those armoured units remains unknown.

Photograph taken in October of 1939 at the Warszawa Zachodnia station (Warsaw West). A reasonable assumption can be made that it is a destroyed combat railcar with 75 mm cannon form improvised armoured train I or II.

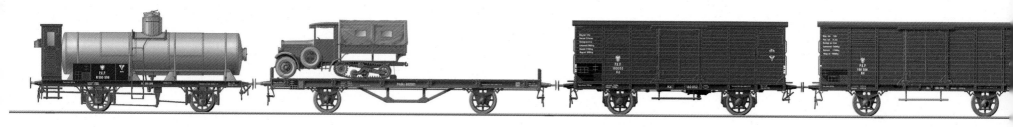

THE AMINISTATIVE SUPPLY TRAINS

Opposite page:
Soldiers of the armoured train P.P. 9 "Marszałek",
around year 1938 during joint exercises of both
Armoured train Groups. Different versions of covered
goods wagons series Kd were used in the administra-
tive supply echelons.

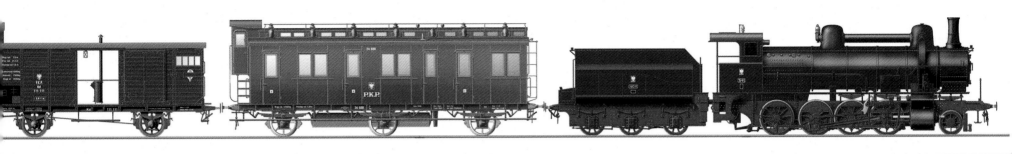

The second, by no means less important part of an armoured train was its administrative detachment. The administrative sections were the logistic support base of the combat trains. Manned by a technical and administrative platoon, they transported food, ammunition supplies, motor vehicles and everything necessary for the efficient operations of the combat train; they also provided resting quarters for the crews of combat sections.

How the administrative trains were put together during the exercises, when the armoured train left the garrison for a longer period of time and during the war mobilization – is not entirely clear. A significant part of the rolling stock was delivered by *P.K.P.* (Polish National Railways). On the eve of the outbreak of the war, the *1. Dywizjon* had 60 *Kd* series covered wagons, one *KK* wagon, eight *Dy* officers' quarter's coaches and nine *Pdk* flat railcars – this number was much lower than the amount needed in case all armoured trains of the unit were to be placed in action. In the *2. Dywizjon*, the situation was even more difficult, because the capacity of the tracks in Niepołomice and Cracow-Bonarka was much smaller.

The mobilization tables for armoured trains have survived, so at least we are aware how an administrative section should be put together – but how was it implemented in practice? Moreover, little or nothing is known about the locomotives of administrative trains and their crews who were often civilian – great pity, because the participation of administrative detachments in the war was no less heroic and worth remembering.

The war rosters from the 1930's differ somewhat in details, and probably, in the end, the actual composition of the trains was determined by the previous practice and the manner of in which *P.K.P.* fulfilled the request for wagons. Reports on exercise travels of armoured trains from the mid-1930's generally mention a steam locomotive, 15 wagons of the *Kd* series and two flat railcars (a flat railcar, for example carrying, a light truck and five *Sokół 1000* motorcycles, or during other exercises, a light truck, three motorcycles and, as part of the wireless set trials, a *Citroen-Kegresse* half-tracked vehicle). There is no precise data in the reports. The hypothetical wartime administrative section was as follows:

Steam Locomotives

The locomotives of the administrative trains were not armoured (hence they were referred to as "black"). In times of peace as well as in case of mobilization, *P.K.P.* supplied the necessary engines.

During peacetime, both Armoured Trains Groups had its own service locomotive used for shunting and other needs of the unit's day to day activities. When the war broke out, and until the evacuation

A volley ball game. In the background, a supply train possibly serving P.P. 2 "Generał Sosnkowski" during summer exercises of the 1. Dywizjon Pociągów Pancernych in 1934.

A quiet afternoon on a portable staircase leading to a Kd series wagon – 2. Dywizjon Pociągów Pancernych in mid 1930's, most likely at Pilawa during summer training.

Soldiers at rest in front of the Kd series wagons of the administrative train from P.P.9 "Marszałek", possibly in 1938.

An auxiliary services locomotive Ti3, inventory number 14 from the Niepołomice based 2nd Armoured Train Group.
Left:
An assembly of the supply train from the 2. Dywizjon Pociągów Pancernych, in mid 1930's. On the right wagon Kd number 184441 of Prussian origin from DOKP Poznań; on the left, a wagon of Austrian provenance originally designated as series Gg.

of the *1. Dywizjon* and the *2. Dywizjon* Reserve Depots, the engines remained at Legionowo and at Cracow-Bonarka sidings respectively. They were not used in administrative section trains and eventually left their garrisons with the last evacuation trains. The *1. Dywizjon* had a locomotive *Ti3* number 6 with tender type *12C1* number 430. The *2. Dywizjon* was assigned with the *Ti3-14* locomotive, also with a 3-axle *12C1* tender, but with an unknown number.

The *P.K.P.* provided the armoured units (and other formations of railway troops) with locomotives of certain types, specially maintained and tested, at the same time ensuring that they were operated by the crews already experienced in the specifics and requirements of the military tasks.

The locomotives for Legionowo were supplied from the resources of *DOKP Warszawa* (National Railways Regional Authority). This region predominantly used steam locomotives of German decent. During the peace period, the railway troops of the Warsaw Corps District typically received *Tp4* locomotives (of German construction, Prussian type *G8¹*, in the resources of *DOKP Warszawa* there were 53 engines in July 1939, and a total of 459 in the *P.K.P.*) and *Tp2* locomotives (of German construction, *G7²* type; in July 1939 there were 80 of them in *DOKP Warszawa*, and in the *P.K.P.* a total of 295 engines). It is reasonable to suppose that the administrative trains formed during mobilization by the *1. Dywizjon* from Legionowo also received such steam engines.

Administrative section trains of the P.P. 52 ("*Śmiały*") and P.P. 53 ("*Piłsud-czyk*") mobilized by the *2. Dywizjon* in 1939 obtained the *Tr11* steam locomotives (Austrian construction, *Type 170*; 50 engines were used under the management of *DOKP Kraków*, and 145 in all by the *P.K.P.*). It is likely that the other armoured trains of the 2nd Armoured Trains Group received the same type of steam locomotives – proven and used in the railway troops since 1918.

The Ti3-14 un-armoured, "black", service locomotive from the Niepołomice base.

The service locomotive of the 1st Armoured Train Group – Ti3-6 with the 12C1 tender number 430 during summer exercises at Czerwony Bór in 1934. The locomotive was used in the Warsaw railway district, mostly electrified by 1930's. The lightning bolt marking painted the steam collection dome and the sand reservoir warned the service crews of electrocution hazard.

An ex Austro-Hungarian locomotive series Tr11 was most commonly used to provide for the military railroad activities in the Cracow Regional Corps district.

A profile of the service locomotive of the 1. Dywizjon Pociągów Pancernych – Prussian made Ti3-6 with 12C1-430 tender.

A profile of the Prussian made Tp2 locomotive with 12C1 tender. The locomotives were frequently used by Warsaw district railway troops.

A profile of an Austro-Hungarian locomotive series 170, renumbered as series Tr11 with 16C11 tender.

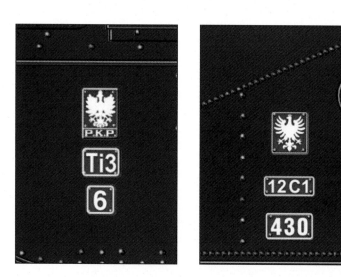

The identifier plaques of the locomotive and the tender. The regulations called for the red background and white lettering. The practice was at times different. Cast bronze, and later brass and zinc alloys were in use.

The crew of the Ti3-14 locomotive – an engineer, an assistant and a fireman – 2. Dywizjon Pociągów Pancernych.

Officers' Living Quarter Coaches

According to the regulations, there would be two *Dy* series coaches in each administrative supply train. Eight such railcars were permanently assigned to the *1. Dywizjon*. The *P.K.P.* supplied the reminder needed for the war needs; they were probably the *Cy* coaches, modified to the standards of the 3rd class passenger carriage, since class the 4th class (signified by letter "D") was eliminated by *P.K.P.* in 1933. The *Dy* railcars serving in the *1. Dywizjon* were numbered 24123, 24645, 24647, 24675, 24690, 24694, 24710 and 24769. In the *2. Dywizjon* of Niepołomice, there were four *Dy* series coaches: 25019, 25079, 25226 and 24959.

The carriages of the *Dy* series in the service of *P.K.P.* were the 4th class (*D*) three-axle (*y*) passenger coaches. They were called *boczniaki* (German name *Abteilwagen*), which meant the entrances to the compartments were from the outside, on both sides, without an internal corridor – an old solution meant to increase the seating space. The wheelbase of the outermost axles was 7.5 – 7.55 m, the overall length of the carriage was 12.2 – 12.4 m, and the weight was approximately 17,500 kg. The carriages had brakeman's cabs and handbrakes, as well as air hoses for Westinghouse brakes.

The coaches were divided into three compartments with an area of approximately 7.6 m² each. Having removed the wooden benches, it was possible to in-stall 1 or 2 beds, a cupboard, a table and a stool. As it seems, six officers were quartered in one coach (two per cabin), while in the other coach – one of the compartments accommodated two officers, and the double compartment was intended for the train commander (this would be indicated by the use of the term "commander's parlour" in one of the reports).

The coaches had electrical installations powered by the Winton generator of the adjacent workshop wagon, while the gas lighting was supplied from an 800 litre tank suspended under the frame. There was steam heating, with steam supplied by a locomotive, from the so-called low pressure steam line.

At times, particularly during longer peacetime training exercises of an armoured train and administrative section, the *Dy* coaches were replaced by the *M* series carriages (symbol *M* – built for military purposes). Occasionally the two axle carriages intended for commanders of ambulance / hospital trains, or two axle ambulance carriages, with officers' quarters and an office compartment were used. The above listed carriages were not just simple, hasty modifications of the 4th class passenger coaches, they were furnished and equipped to offer an incomparably better comfort.

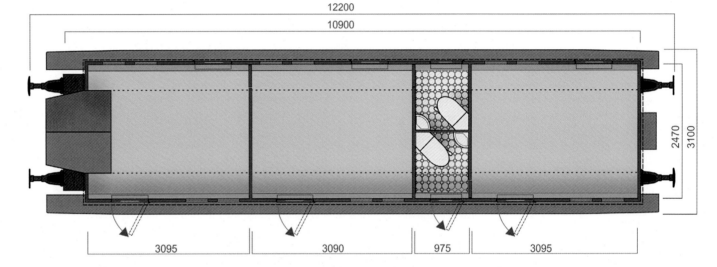

An outline of the living quarters in the German designed "Abteilwagen". After the removal of the benches, three sizable – about 7,6 meters square each – compartments were available.

An enlargement of a photograph's background – thus a poor quality image – depicting one of the officers' coaches in the 2nd Armoured Trains Group at Niepołomice, circa 1934.

A profile of an officers' quarters carriage series Dy number 25226 from the 2. Dywizjon Pociągów Pancernych.

A profile of an officers' quarters coach series Dy number 24690 from the 1. Dywizjon Pociągów Pancernych.

Soldiers of the "Generał Sosnkowski" – in the background a military purpose wagon series Mhx.

Troops' Living Quarter Wagons

The standard two axle covered goods wagons of the *Kd* series were intended as sleeping quarters for the troops (symbol *K* – covered, 2 or 3-axle wagon; symbol *d* – load capacity from 15,000 to less than 20,000 kg). Less often, the *Km* series covered wagons with a load capacity of less than 15,000 kg were used (in the interwar period some of the *Km* wagons had been rebuild and strengthened to carry 15 to 16 tons of load, which placed them in the *Kd* designation). However, due to their smaller load area, they were much less suitable to arrange for the transport of troops (in general, the *Km* wagons set aside by the *P.K.P.* regional districts "for use by the military authorities" were decaying on the sidings without any use and maintenance).

The *Kd* series wagons were of various origins – from the old German and Prussian railways, the Austro-Hungarian railways, small quantities from the Russian railways (after conversion to the standard European gauge), and finally, Polish issue from Cegielski Plant at Poznań, Lilpop, Rau & Loewenstein of Warsaw, *Huta Ostrowiecka...* and other manufacturers.

Contrary to the appearances, the diversity did not cause major logistical difficulties. The Prussian Railways implemented the standardization of the roll-

An administrative supply train – two Kd wagons of Polish or German construction followed by two Austrian ones.

Another view of the supply echelon with Kd wagons – the first one, either Polish or German, followed by an ex k.k.St.B., Austrian one.

A commemorative photograph of the 2. Dywizjon in front of the ex Austrian Gg series wagon, renumbered as Kd 150054.

ing stock at the end of the 19th century. Over time, the regulations were perfected and introduced to all German railways. Consequently, most European countries adopted the well construed German norms. The Polish-built railway wagons did not differ much from German types. The normative *C-I* standard – according to which the Polish *Kd* wagons were built, was modelled after the German *A2* covered goods wagon (*Bedeckte Güterwagen Gm*, the so-called union type), which was based on the earlier Prussian *IId8* design.

A typical *Kd* railcar was a two axle (three axle variants were rare as they were a reminiscence of the bygone era) wagon, with the wheelbase usually being 4.5 m, and the length of the loading area extending 7 to 8 m. The sliding doors were 1.5 m wide (in some ex-Austrian wagons a few centimetres more). The wagons permanently assigned to the Armoured Train Groups were often equipped with the so called cargo gate inserts – a panel with personnel entry door, often glazed, and two window panes replacing the ventilation openings. Additional door and window inserts intended for wagons supplied by *P.K.P.* were stored in the mobilization reserve magazines.

Each administrative section train had a minimum of eight troop quarters *Kd* series wagons. Each wagon could accommodate 16 soldiers (maximum of 20, depending on the actual size of the loading area). The beds were three tier bunks with mattresses filled with seaweed grass (rather than hay typically used for infantry transport echelons). The remaining equipment consisted of cupboards (with 8 to 12 individual compartments), quar-

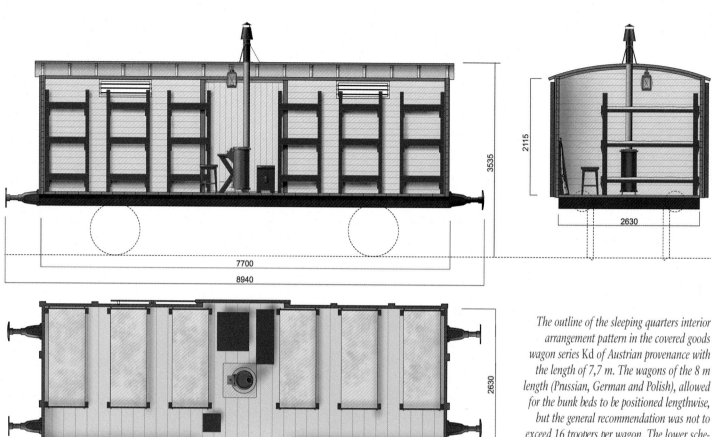

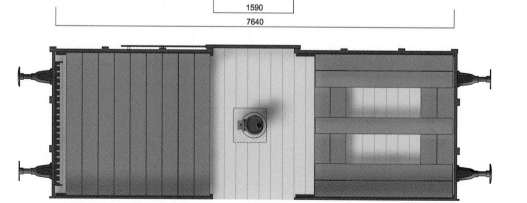

The outline of the sleeping quarters interior arrangement pattern in the covered goods wagon series Kd of Austrian provenance with the length of 7,7 m. The wagons of the 8 m length (Prussian, German and Polish), allowed for the bunk beds to be positioned lengthwise, but the general recommendation was not to exceed 16 troopers per wagon. The lower schematic illustrates the arrangement of the wagon for ordinary troop transport with the use of the boards consisting of a regulatory wagon equipment. During regular commercial service the boards were carried on special hangers at the end walls.

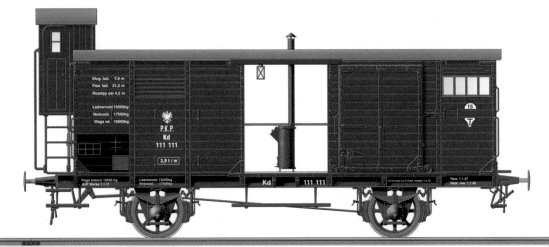

A profile of the Kd wagon adopted for troop sleeping purposes. The brake equipped wagon is of German construction referred to as type 118D. There is a four pane glass insert in place of a ventilation panel. Instead of a door insert, there is a horizontal safety bar – a wooden rod with steel sleeves. The heating stove does not have a typical protective housing.

In the background, a Kd 187382 wagon in 1935. The wagon is of German provenance from DOKP Poznań. The wagon has a cargo gate door insert and a window insert in place of the ventilation louvers.

termaster's cabinet, gas mask storage cabinet, rifle rack, a table and a bench, coat hangers and a fire extinguisher.

The heating, according to regulations to be in use between 15 November and 15 April, was provided by the means of a heating stove placed on an asbestos and metal base bolted down to the floor, with the sheet metal shield also affixed to the floor. The fumes were evacuated by an upright pipe of 12 cm diameter. The roof opening was protected by a layer of asbestos and sheet metal. The wagons supplied by P.K.P. more often than not had an existing opening in the roof covered with sheet metal hood. The regulation allowed 20 kilogram of coal per day, but in extreme cold conditions additional supply could have been obtained from the locomotive's tender.

The wagons were equipped with electrical installation, but in absence of the locomotive or the lack of the repair shop wagon equipped with portable generator, a regulation candle lamps were in use.

German built Kd wagon number 191321. A cargo gate door insert without window and unusual window insert may be noticed.

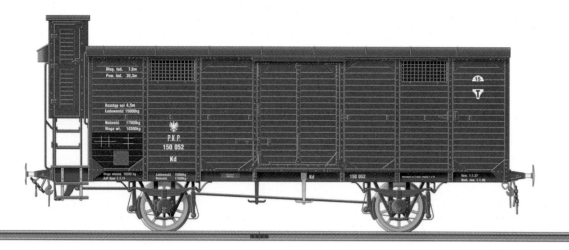

Colour profile of the series Kd covered wagon with brake system of Austrian origin. The interior load length was 7,9 m.

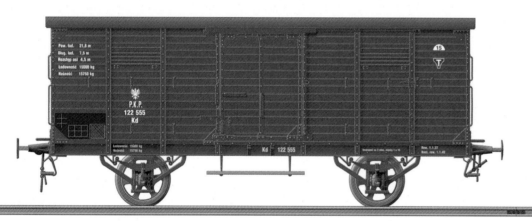

A profile of a compatible, Prussian made Kd wagon originally designated as Blatt IIb3.

A regulation, wooden safety rod with steel sleeves and mounting chains used when a cargo wagon was used to transport persons. The end brackets were easily mounted to the frame of the cargo gate.

Typical coal heating stove used in troop transport wagons. The P.K.P. was obligated to provide this equipment with the rolling stock, but a reserve w also kept at the warehouses of the Armoured Train Groups.

A usual smokestack used with the heating stoves. The shapes varied but two kinds were in use a 12 cm diameter tube for heating and 15 cm diameter for kitchen stoves.

A typical candle lantern – considered as a required equipment of the covered wagons supplied by P.K.P. for military use.

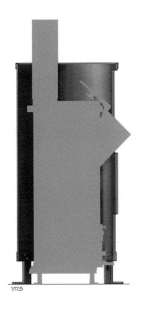

1/17,5

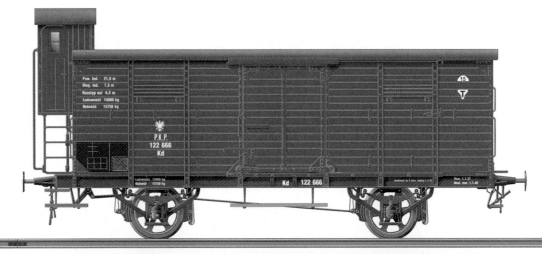

A profile of a Prussian origin Kd wagon with brakes and brakeman's cab, originally designated as Blatt IIb3.

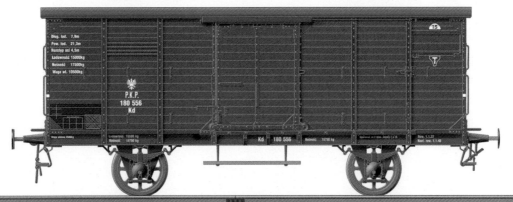

A profile of a German built Kd wagon (designated as Blatt A2 and Polish version as type C-I).

Cross section drawing of a typical shield made to prevent burning in case of direct contact with hot surface of the stove.

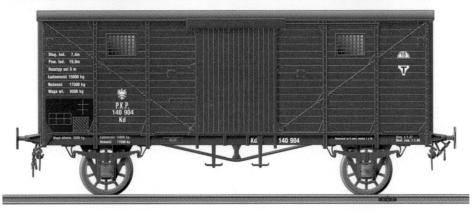

A profile of a Hungarian built Kd wagon with the loading lengths of 7,5 m.

Non Commissioned Officers' Living Quarter Wagons

There were also two *Kd* series wagons intended for NCO's. The layout and equipment was similar to the troop wagons, but the level of comfort was a little higher as only 14 NCO's occupied one wagon.

An interior of the Kd wagon – soldiers at the table.

The sleeping quarters Kd wagon from "Marszałek" of the 2. Dywizjon – the edges of the bunk beds arrangement are visible. In this configuration the beds were aligned with the side walls of the wagon.

A Kd series wagon number 188851 of German construction dispatched from the DOKP Poznań, in the 2. Dywizjon supply echelon.

A Kd wagon most likely of Polish production. The Westing-house air brake system may be noticed. There is also a door inset. Photo of "Marszałek" during exercises.

A rather uncommon scenario, a small Km series wagon in the assembly of the "Generał Sosnkowski" supply echelon in 1934.

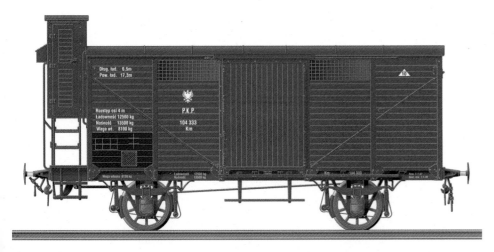

The Km series wagon with hand brake and brakemen's cabin. Wagons of this type were mostly built by Hungarian rail yards, and were commonly used throughout the k.u.k. Empire. The loading length was 6,5 m.

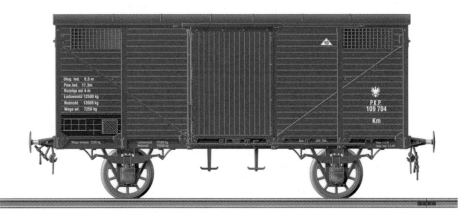

The Km series wagon without brakes.

A photograph of a Km wagon without brakes.

The Km series wagon with different arrangement of the ventilation panels.

Administration Wagon

Typically, the administration office was housed in a standard *Kd* series wagon. On some occasions the *P.K.P.* would supply a *Kp* series wagon commercially used for transport lightweight but large volume cargo. This type of railcar was mainly manufactured by *Huta Ostrowiecka* on the under-frame of the typical *Pdks* flat railcar. The interior length was 13 meters, and the load area 35,5 m² – that was almost 15 m² more than a typical *Kd* wagon.

The adaptation of the wagon was done by installing a partition, with a door, dividing the interior into two areas – the larger as an actual administration office, and a smaller intended as living quarters of a sergeant-chief and a quartermaster NCO. The living section had two beds, an armoire, a table and two stools. An office section was equipped with two desks, chairs, filing cabinet, supply cabinet, phone shelf, a wall clock and other office equipment including a typewriter.

The lighting was electric – two light fixtures in the office and one in the sleeping room, but there were, of course, the backup candle lamps.

The administration office in a typical Kd wagon. Photograph taken at the 2ⁿᵈ Armoured Train Group.

"Kancelaria" – an administration office in a Kd wagon at 1ˢᵗ Armoured Train Group during gunnery practice in Rembertów in 1929.

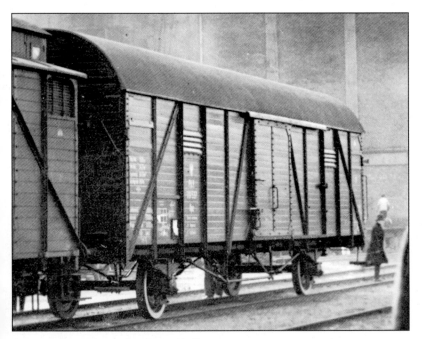

A two-axle large cargo capacity wagon series Kp.

Wagon Kp as an administrative office of the 2nd Armoured train Group in 1934 at Pilawa. Behind a small draisine of unknown type in camouflage paint, and the prototype of the self propelled artillery wagon (one of the last existing photographs as the wagon was dissembled that same year).

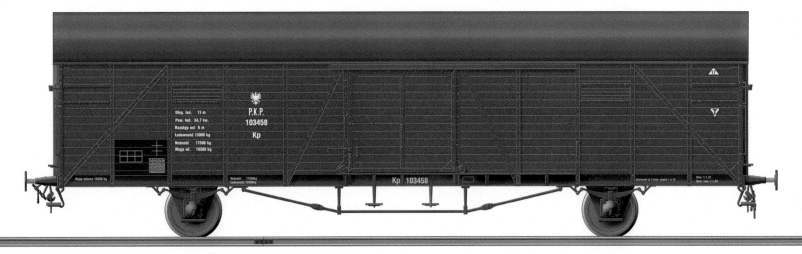

A profile of a Kp wagon often used for furniture transport build by "Huta Ostrowiec".

Sick-bay Paramedic Wagon

The "ambulance wagon" was an alternate term for the *Kd* series wagon equipped with standard gate insert panel providing a personnel entry door.

In a basic version, the partition divided the interior of the wagon into two separate spaces. A pharmaceutical section with apothecary supplies and instruments, and a larger treatment room for the wounded. In the pharmacy compartment there were medicine cabinets, a table, and a suspended water tank supplying a small sink. The treatment room had an operating table, surgery instruments cabinet and a second sink.

In some cases the conversion of *Kd* series wagon for medical purposes was more sophisticated. The interior was still divided by the partition, and the gate insert personnel door panels were also put in place, but glass window panes (upper segment could be lowered for ventilation) measuring some 50 x 75 cm were installed in both side walls of the wagon. The treatment room, as in the basic version, had an operating table, surgery instruments cabinet and a sink, but also a bed for the paramedic on duty.

The second compartment served as an actual sick-bay – with three beds and all other necessary furnishings.

The lighting was electric, as in other wagons, with backup candle lamps and electrical battery portable lanterns.

Kitchen Wagon

The kitchen wagon was a typical *Kd* covered goods van adopted for the purpose by removal of the upper side boards (ventilation purposes) and a cut-out in the roof to accommodate the 15 cm diameter smoke stack of the stove. The stove was an enlarged version of a typical heating stove capable of warming a large pot. There was an anchored frame designed to secure the standard military field kitchen. The cooking equipment was complemented by a large chef's table with a zinc top, a side table, a cupboard, pot hangers, and a stool with a basin for meat cleaning purposes. A separate section of the kitchen wagon was sometimes used for food pantry. On some occasions the provisions were carried in a dedicated *Kd* or *Km* series wagon, however the regulations did not require this – the assignment was done at the train's commander discretion.

An improvised kitchen on a Pd type flat railcar with wooden stanchions during 1934 exercises of the 1st Armoured Train Group.

Repair Shop Wagon

The shop wagon was also divided into two compartments, an actual workshop and supply storage (it is not known if such wagons were present in all echelons, but it would have been a *Kd* series covered goods wagon). In fact, the *Kd* series was too small so the Armoured Train Group officers suggested the use of a dedicated *KK* series railcar – a long, large capacity four axle type – in order to better equip and thus expand the repair capacities in the field. It is unlikely that the proposal was implemented before the war (*1. Dywizjon* had only one *KKz* wagon on the roster as of 1 January 1939). The shop crew consisted of a tank mechanic, automobile mechanic (with electrical qualifications), machinist, welder, blacksmith, cannoneer and a gunsmith.

The shop compartment was equipped with a workbench, tool storage cabinet and a portable forging hearth (to be used outside of the wagon). An important item was a Winton portable generator providing 110 V current (it is uncertain if the armoured groups were able to complete the replacement of the ageing original engines with the new *Polish Fiat 508* units). The generator provided electricity for the train and was used to charge batteries.

Fuel Storage Wagon

Again, a *Kd* series wagon. The fuel and oils were stored in drums placed on special frames bolted down to the floor boards. The fuel wagons were to be without brakes, but if not available, the brakes were to be disabled (safety concern with sparking). The equipment consisted of a table, a stool, inventory board and an electrical lantern. The electrical installation was not used due to safety concerns.

Technical, Uniform and Portable Firearms Storage Wagon

The wagon was also a *Kd* series covered goods railcar. It was equipped with a table, a stool, inventory board and an electrical lantern.

Ammunition Storage Wagon

Two *Kd* covered goods wagons positioned at the end of the train to allow emergency uncoupling. The wagons carried ammunition, explosives and fuses. The wagons were not supposed to have active breaks. The standard storage wagon equipment – a table, a stool, an inventory board and an electrical lantern were provided. The electrical installation was not used.

A portable 5 kW electrical generator Winton *with an original 8 horse power gasoline engine.*

Above and right:
A portable electrical generator Winton, *modified by installation of a P.Z.Inż. 108 engine.*

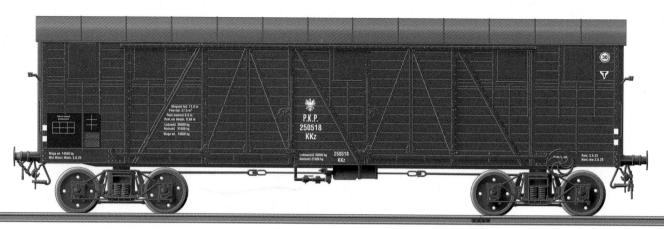

KKz wagon. The American made wagons had proven themselves as a successful adaptation for a mechanical workshop at the railway bridges companies and were considered for use with the Armoured Train Groups.

The four axle KKz wagons with air brake installation.

Flat Railcars

The flatcars transported the motor vehicles (according to regulations: a passenger car, two 2 ton capacity trucks, one above 2 ton capacity truck and a motorcycle with a sidecar – in practice, a varying array, for example two to three motorcy-cles and two half tracked trucks *wz.34* with rail-guides). If available, a spare *TK* tankette, a hand operated rail draizine, unloading ramps, rails and railroad ties were also carried.

The *1. Dywizjon* had 12 *Pdk* flat railcars as the mobilization reserve (not including the *Pdks* flatcars intended for combat trains). In the *2. Dywizjon* there were 10 *Pdk* and two *Pddk* flatcars (also not including the *Pdks* flatcars). During mobilization *P.K.P.* mostly supplied the 15 ton cargo capacity *Pdk* with only a few 20 ton capacity *Pddk* flat railcars. Cargo chains and wheel blocks had to be supplied with each. The larger *PPk* series flatcars were not needed, but it can not be ruled out that some four axle ones were used during September Campaign.

The low sided Pdk *flat railcars with wooded stanchions. The photograph documents the exercises of the 2. Dywizjon at Pilawa, in 1934 (in the background both Tatra draisines covered with tarpaulins).*

A low sided Pddk flat railcar with wooded stanchions.

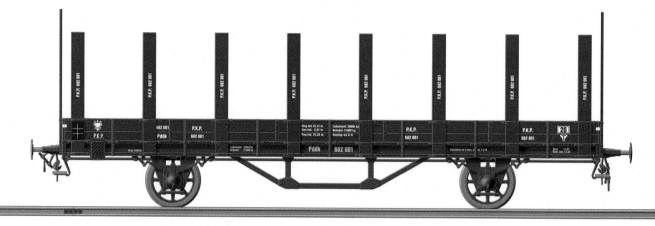

A Pdk flat railcar, without brakes, manufactured by Zieleniewski factory at Sanok according to the Polish pattern C-IV.

A Pddkz flat railcar manufactured by Cegielski factory at Poznań.

A Pddkz, with hand operated brake and brakeman's, equipped with steel stanchions.

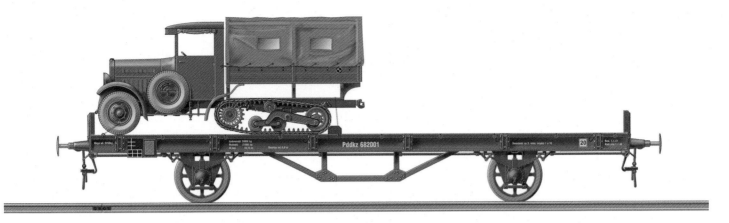

An outline of Pddkz flat railcar with the stanchions removed carrying a wz. 34 half track.

A front of a Pdks flat railcar and a provisional loading ramp constructed form railroad sleepers (tie) and rails.

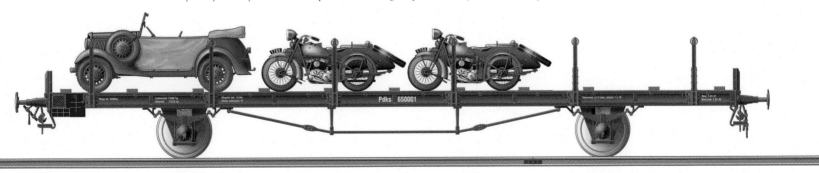

A Pdks railcar of Prussian origin with steel stanchions and front boards. An all terrain Polski Fiat 508 "Łazik" and two Sokół 1000 motorcycles transported.

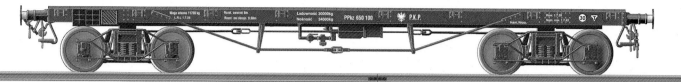

A American made PPkz with the sideboards and the stanchions removed.

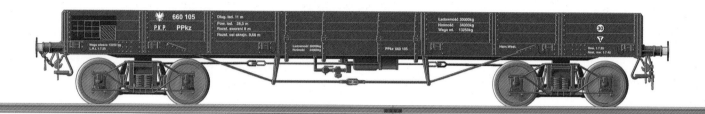

A American made PPkz with the sideboards but with the stanchions removed.

An American made 4 axle flat railcar series PPkz with air brake system.

Coal Wagon

The open wagon carried an "iron reserve" coal for the locomotives of the armoured train and the supply echelon. In 1939 the *P.K.P.* had over 70 thousand open wagons of various types. They were predominantly 15 ton *Wd* and 20 ton cargo capacity *Wdd* series. They were acquired from diverse sources, pre World War One Austro-Hungarian origin wagons from Austrian, Czech and Hungarian manufactures, Prussian and German, as well as a large number of modern coal railcars of Polish construction.

Typical Polish markings on the side of the commercial freight wagon.

Romanian military delegation during a visit at Legionowo, in 1.Dywizjon. The presentation of draisine equipment – TK rail guides and R tank transports is depicted. In the background, there is an Austrian open goods wagon series Jk h

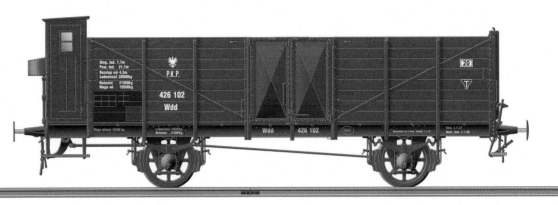

A profile of a series Wdd (20 ton capacity) German built coal wagon type IId2, with hand brake and brakeman's cabin.

Polish made Wddz with hand brake and brakeman's cab, but also with the air brake hose.

New Wddz coal wagons without brakes but equipped with air brake connection hoses.

A Wddz of Polish manufacture according the specification CIIa.

A Wdk open wagon of Austrian manufacture, originally used as series Jk h.

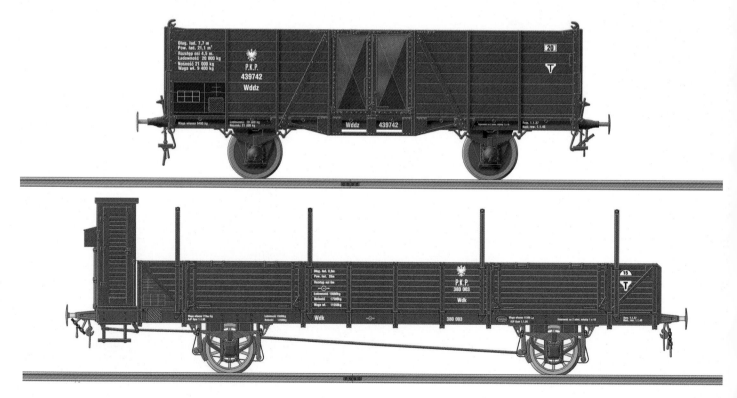

Tanker Wagon

The tank wagons used in commercial traffic to transport fuels – gasoline, oil and kerosene were used to carry water reserve for locomotives of the armoured trains. No special preparations were needed as the steam engine water did not have to be pure.

A tank wagon and a Kd wagon from the administrative echelon coupled to the trailing flat railcar of "Generał Sosnkowski". Both wagon remained unaffected by the explosion and were quickly hauled away by the Germans.

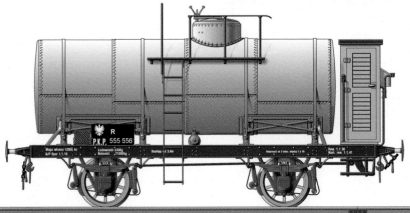

A tanker wagon with hand brake and brakeman's cab of Austrian origin.

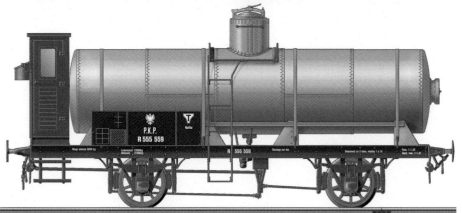

A different version of Austrian tanker wagon.

An aerial view of the tank wagon and a Kd wagon from "Generał Sosnkowski".

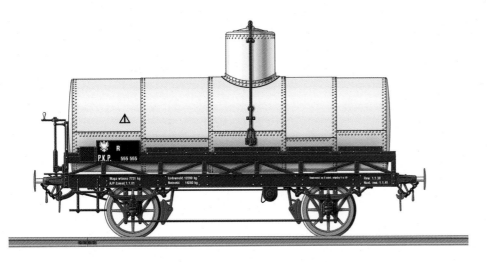

A Russian tank wagon converted to run on European track.

Guards Van

Some of the accounts of September Campaign indicate a presence of a wagon assigned as a guard post, not required by the regulations. However, particularly in case of loosing contact with the combat train, self defence of the supply echelon would be of significance.

The self protection aspect was never quite resolved. The anti aerial defence was particularly important. Typical set of three tripod mounted machine guns carried on the flat railcars was insufficient due to the limited traverse of fire. In 1936, the *1. Dywizjon* begun developing a concept of a conversion kit which was an anti aircraft machine gun emplacement installed in place of the typical brakeman's cab. The project was under way at the *B.B. Tech Br. Panc.* (Bureau of Technical Development of Armoured Forces) and the prototype was to be made at the *1. Dywizjon* workshop and tested during the summer manoeuvres of 1939. There is no information in regards to the details of the project.

In the middle of the photograph, a tanker wagon belonging to Polmin Factory from Jasło at the refinery in Drohobycz. It is the same type, Austrian provenance, wagon as used in "Generał Sosnkowski".

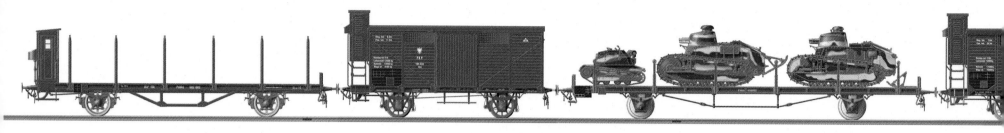

THE EVACUATION TRAINS

The bombardment of railway lines was a strategically important function of German Luftwaffe, but the attacks on the stations, the railway hubs and individual trains (including passenger and medical) was even more devastating.

The First Evacuation Train of the 2nd Armoured Train Group

On the evening of 1 September an order was issued to evacuate the headquarters as well as the wife's and families of the officers. During the course of the night on 4 September, at 4 o'clock in the morning, the train left Podłęże station. En route, the train was attacked by enemy airplanes. Without any significant damage, it reached Tarnobrzeg, a destination planned for a provisional training base. As it turned out, the buildings designated to house the personnel were bombed and completely devastated; the centre of the town was engulfed in flames. The subsequent air raid destroyed the train stationed at the Tarnobrzeg railroad siding, so the passengers were loaded on the trucks and left for Romanian border, traveling through Sandomierz, Lwów, Brody, Stanisławów and Kołomyja. After prolonged wait, without any shelter, the people were allowed to cross into Romania on 19 September 1939.

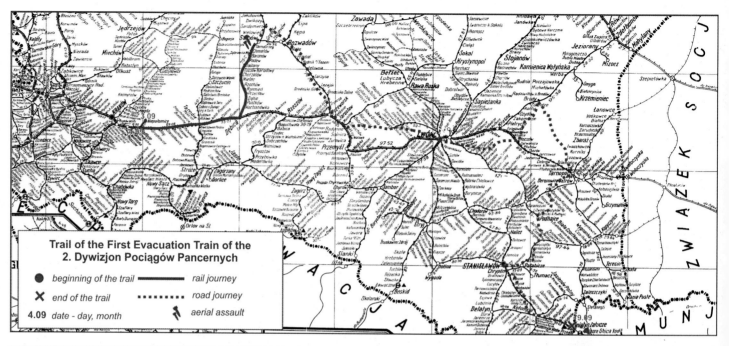

Trail of the First Evacuation Train of the 2. Dywizjon Pociągów Pancernych

● beginning of the trail   ——— rail journey

✕ end of the trail   ···· road journey

4.09 date - day, month   aerial assault

The autumn of 1939; Tarnów station on the Kraków – Lwów railway line. The evacuation trains of the 2nd Armoured Train Group left from Niepołomice, and travelled east trough Podłęże and Tarnów.

The Second Evacuation Train of the 2nd Armoured Train Group

The evacuation of the 2nd Armoured Train Group's base was ordered on 4 of September. Captain Bronisław Konieczny, Group's paymaster, was assigned as a commanding officer. Around noon of that day *P.K.P.* (Polish National Railways) supplied open wagons alongside some flat railcars. Covered goods wagons were not available, as they were already dispositioned for other missions. This obviously provided a challenge, as many materials needed protection against weather elements. Tarps and other improvised covers were utilized to protect the load. The composition of the train was as follows:
- medical supplies and operating equipment – one wagon (one officer's family evacuating late was tucked along).
- uniforms and other quartermaster's materials – two wagons.
- food rations – two wagons.
- live stock – one wagon.
- armament and munitions – one wagon.
- divisional store (and a few more families of the troops) – one wagon.
- technical equipment and materials for the armoured vehicles – two wagons.
- registrar, archives and documents – one wagon.
- field kitchen (old tsarist model), motorcycles and one disabled cross terrain car – two flat wagons.

The following four open wagons accommodated 130 active duty soldiers and reservists, some cadets, 10 non commissioned officers and 15 civilian employees of the Armoured Group. The train was supplemented by two seemingly abandoned open wagons with a load of coal; after arrival at Podłęże station, four wagons with track repair materials were added. In all, the evacuation echelon consisted of 23 wagons. The service locomotive of the 2nd Armoured Train Group – *Ti3-14* was used to take the evacuation train to Podłęże.

On the morning of 5 September the evacuation train was coupled with an empty express train heading towards Lwów via Tarnów. It had to be enforced, using the provisions of the marshal law. Some additional wagons carrying the personnel of Niepołomice and Podłęże stations were added to the train. After just a few kilometers, the train had to stop and wait for removal of the wreckage caused by the collision of two preceding trains.

The next delay took place right before the Słotwina Brzeska station due to track damage. The train was attacked by three German planes, but there was a machine gun available for anti-aerial defense. The losses were minimal, which can not be said about transports stopped in front of the echelon. The crew assisted in transporting the wounded to the medical train, also stuck in a jam a few hundred yards behind.

During the night of 5 September the track repair at Słotwina was successfully carried out so the train was able to advance to Bogumiłowice. The right track, on which the train traveled, was com-

The autumn of 1939; the destruction at the Jarosław station.

Some of the obstacles were impossible to remove by limited means of train crews just like this overturned locomotive.

pletely blocked by transports heading east. The echelon was able to back up to the crossing switch and continue the journey using the left railroad track.

The next stop was at Tarnów where it became apparent that the massive traffic jam was caused by the lack of water at the pumps. Eventually, at the great expense of effort, the water in the locomotives was partially replenished using buckets, so a few of the stuck trains, including the evacuation echelon, were able to advance past Tarnów to the functioning water pump. During the service stop some one hundred wounded were placed in the empty carriages of the express train hauling the echelon. Bound by their obligations, the soldiers of the 2nd Armoured Train Group had to provide care for the wounded as no one else was available for this task. On 7 September the train continued to Dębica and eventually arrived at Tarnobrzeg. The siding at the station became a resting stop as the commander tried to make contact with divisional headquarters to obtain new directives. It was decided to continue to Żurawica along the line Rozwadów – Przeworsk – Przemyśl. Another track repair and removal of damaged railway wagons became necessary. In the afternoon of 8 September the echelon was able to continue towards Rozwadów where jet another jam was encountered. A number of transport trains set idle due to lack of water. Again, the troops of the 2nd Armoured Train Group and a few hundred civilians stood up to the challenge organizing a chain delivery system using buckets, and whatever available containers, to carry water from a nearby pond.

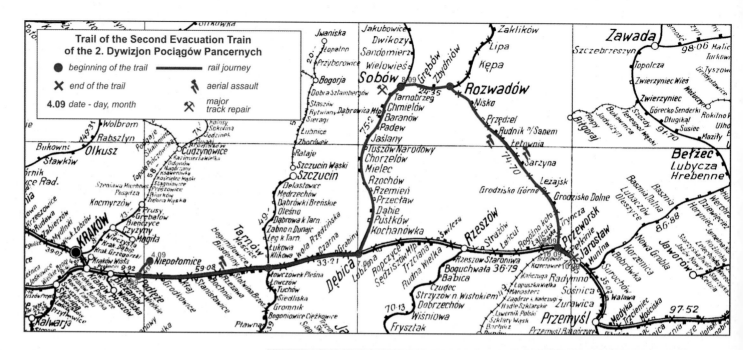

After four hours the trains were again on the move. Another stop had to be taken at Rozwadów station, the coal and water were available, but the trains had to wait their turn to replenish the fuel. In the evening the echelon was able to continue south-east. At Nisko station more water and coal were restocked just in case of shortages ahead. The railroad track toward Leżajsk was in poor condition so the train had to move slowly; thus, it was so much vulnerable to German air attacks. The crew put up a defence using the only available machine gun and rifles. Przeworsk station was reached in the afternoon of 9 September. The train left Przeworsk in the morning 10 September.

Destroyed coal wagons blocking the tracks.

About four kilometres before, another stop had to be made due to the damage to the bridge. Some two hundred meters away, on the other track, there was an armoured exercise train evacuated from the base at Niepołomice, also stuck in the jam. At some point in the afternoon, the exercise train engaged an approaching German tank and armoured car column. The echelon troops assumed defensive positions and used their sole machine gun to provide support in this uneven skirmish. But, this was an end – the crew abandoned the evacuation echelon as it was set ablaze during the fight.

The Exercise Train of the Reserve Detachment of the 2nd Armoured Train Group

As the combat trains left for the front, the base at Niepołomice begun to assemble a training unit – Armoured Exercise Train. The crew consisted mostly of cadets from the divisional NCO academy. Upon completion of field training they were to reinforce the frontline crews.

Captain Franciszek Pietrzak was nominated as a commander (Lieutenant Michał Gawroński [?] became the second in command). The crew consisted of about 60 men.

Rapid advances of the German Army resulted in a decision to dispatch the train towards Tarnobrzeg where the Training Centre of the Reserve Troops was to be established. It appears (only a few photographs of the destroyed train are available) that the train was composed as follows:
– in the front there were three flat wagons series *Pdks*. The first two carried a *TKS* tankette (the leading flat wagon had a *TKS*, the second possibly a *TK-3*, but more likely also a *TKS*) and two *Renault FT* tanks each (the tanks seem to be missing armament; possibly the surplus tanks delivered in the last days of August). The third flat wagon was loaded with a *Sokół 1000* motorcycle with side car, a field kitchen and probably a third tankette.
– two covered goods wagons, most likely of a Austro-Hungarian decent (the brakeman's cabs are smaller than in German, and later Polish wagons).

The five freight wagons were followed by:
– series *Ti3-14* un-armoured locomotive used for service in the 2nd Armoured Train Group (original German designation 4024 Posen, manufactured by *BMAG* in 1904, factory number 3384 with a *12C1* tender of an unknown number).

The locomotive was followed by:
– freight covered goods wagon *Kd* series with breaks.
– a pair of two axle artillery armoured wagons, armed with 75 mm field guns, numbers 398624 and 398625 (former wagons of the 1st Armoured Train Group, modified in 1930's).
– assault wagon 430043; former wagon of "Stefan Czarniecki" dating back to the early 1920's composition of that train. There was a characteristic observation cupola installed on the roof, it was removed from one of the locomotives retrofitted with the "*Ursus*" type turret. The wagon was not equipped with radio communications equipment.
– artillery wagon number 630727, two axle "warsaw" type (original number 02006) armed with 100 mm howitzer.

One of the written accounts indicates the presence of the *R* type rail guide draisine preceding the train, stating that its tank fired the first shot at the German ar-

An artillery wagon of the Exercise Train armed with the howitzer – "warsaw" type wagon on the Russian chassis number 02006, assigned a new number 630727. The wagon is modified – fitted with machine gun turret and wz.14 howitzer. The camouflage pattern is typical the beginning of 1930's. There is a fragment of a covered wagon visible on the left. The wagon number Kd 137544 was permanently assigned to the 2. Dywizjon and was stationed at Bonarka siding.

moured column at the battle of Jarosław. The above relation is questionable.

The armoured train did not have an independent administrative support train attachment (thus the freight wagons included in its composition).

Departure of the Exercise Train (*Pociąg Szkolny Ośrodka Zapasowego*) from Niepołomice took place on 5 September at 15:00 hours. At about 20:00 hours the train reached Bochnia. There was a roadblock ahead, two transport trains sat idle as the water supply in the locomotives was depleted. The exercise train was able to push both disabled transports to the railroad crossing at Dębica and then headed north-east to Tarnobrzeg arriving on 7 September at about 18:00 hours. At 22:00 hours an order came dispatching the Exercise Armoured Train to Lwów.

In the afternoon of 9 September the train successfully fended off an attack of German air force, but the rail track ahead was damaged. The repair was conducted by the crew, allowing the train to reach Przeworsk at 6 o'clock in the morning of 10 September.

The rail line Przeworsk – Przemyśl was completely blocked by stalled evacuation transport trains. On the approach to Jarosław station, the ability of further advance ended.

At around 16:00 hours (according to another account at 14:00) a German armoured unit came in sight. According to the account provided by the commander, the train open fire from the gun and a howitzer. In effect, some five to seven German tanks and armoured cars were destroyed (another, previously stated account, claims that the *R* draisine completely destroyed one of German vehicles, however the observer was some 200 meters away, thus the relation is questionable).

At approximately 17:00 hours the Germans were able to bring in, and position, a battery of field guns to shell the armoured train. At that point the train become defenceless as the parallel track, facing the enemy field guns, was filled with abandoned transports, limiting the traverse of fire to the gaps between the immobilized wagons. Two hours later, at 19:00 hours, Captain Pietrzak issued an order to abandon the train. The crew were able to unload and salvage two of the tankettes (a photograph of the abandoned train shows a makeshift ramp). After the crew left the train, the certified tank personnel joined the 10th Motorised Cavalry Brigade on 12 September.

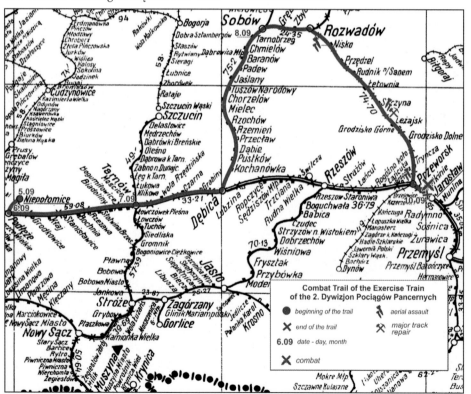

The Exercise Train – flat railcar Pdks with a TKS tankette and two Renault FT. By the next railcar carrying same cargo, a provisional loading ramp is visible.

Next page: A situational sketch made by platoon leader Tadeusz Zegan from the workshop detachment.

There is another, quite credible, account of the events that followed. According to the relation, after the departure order was issued, a group of the artillery men returned to the train. The howitzer artillery wagon was damaged by German artillery fire in such a way that the front wheel set was pushed backwards, allowing the dislodged turret to settle on the track in an upright position. The muzzle of the howitzer remained pointed to gap between the disabled locomotives (a *Tr11* locomotive and a freight wagon as the photographs seem to indicate). The artilleryman opened fire towards the six German tanks visible through the gap. Aiming "along the barrel" due to the short range, they were able to score three direct hits destroying the German tanks.

On the left track, remnants of the howitzer wagon, assault wagon, followed by two artillery wagons with 75 mm cannons. Burned out coal wagon and abandoned Tr11 locomotive occupy the right track. Below: A close up.

1. Railway station Pełkinie
2. Steam locomotives from Płaszów
3. Armoured train "Naprzód" ("Ahead")
4. Armoured draisine
5. Workshop detachment of the evacuation train
6. Supplies wagons of the evacuation train
7. Broken railroad tracks
8. Country farm
9. Enemy machine gun position
10. Country farm
11. Haystack
12. German tanks
13. Manor buildings
14. Enemy artillery
15. The enemy's first salvo
16. A plate fallen from an armoured train

Attention. Only combat objects are marked on the railroad track. In fact, the railroad tracks were clogged with evacuation trains, so any movement of the armoured train was impossible.

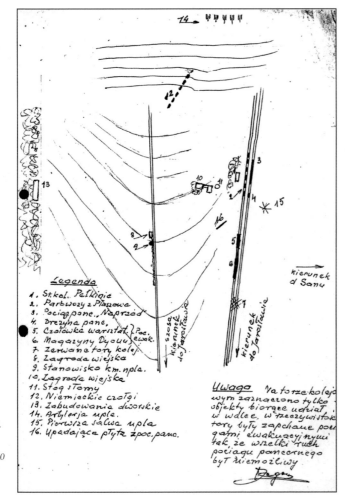

Previous page:
The destroyed Exercise Train – a fragment of the assault wagon and remnants of the blown up howitzer wagon.

An assault wagon number 430043 and both 75 mm artillery wagons – on the right number 398625, in the middle number 398624.

On the right:
Autumn of 1939, the combat wagons of Exercise Train are still at Pełkinie but the destroyed rolling stock is already removed.

A "commemorative" photograph of German soldiers posed by wagon 398624; on the right, corner of wagon number 398625.

A profile of locomotive Ti3-14 *serving as auxiliary engine of the* 2. Dywizjon.

Assault wagon 430043.

Pdks *flat railcar with a* TKS *tankette and two* Renault *tanks.*

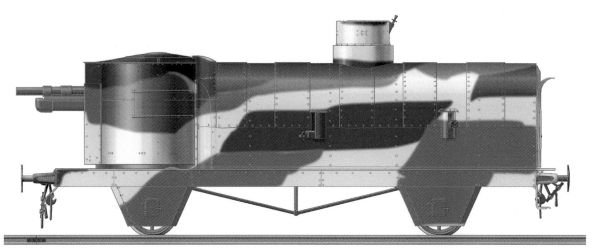

A profile of artillery wagon 636727 – the paint scheme may have been a little different.

Photograph taken September 18 1939. A TKS tankette on the road near Jarosław. In the background, a viaduct and the embankment of the Kraków – Lwów railway line. It is likely the tankette came from the Exercise Train, but it is unclear why was it abandoned so close to the tracks.

To the right:
Artillery wagon number 398624 in German service with Panzerzug 21 mostly composed from Polish equipment. The wagon is already somewhat modified – Westinghouse airbrake system and a small apron protecting the air reservoir are added, but the camouflage pattern is still original.

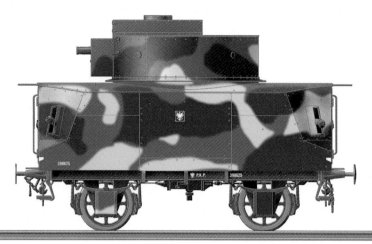

A profile of artillery wagon 398625.

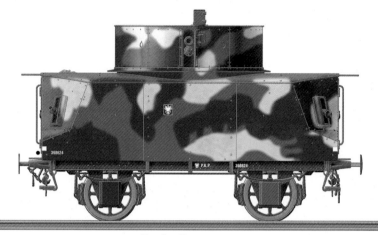

A profile of artillery wagon 398624.

Three photographs of the German Panzerzug 22 wagon, previously Polish 398625 – repainted and modified by adding running gear protective aprons.

Previous page: Partial view of Panzerzug 22 – ex Polish artillery wagon 398625 followed by an assault wagon from PP.52 " Piłsudczyk".

The Evacuation Train of the 1st Armoured Train Group

The "remnants of the Armoured Group" – not a very graceful description used to identify the surplus munitions and personnel left after the military unit mobilized its resources for the front lines. The original mobilization rosters required the 1st Armoured Train Group to form a Reserve Detachment of the Railway Troops No. 1 and assemble an armoured train for combat training purposes. The intent was to train the recruits in order to replenish operational losses at the front lines.

The 1st Armoured Train Group was not able to field such a train – there was no equipment left. The two *R* draisines left over after the front line units departed, were assigned to patrol and secure the rail line between Wieliszewo and Warszawa until the departure of the evacuation trains of the 1st Armoured Train Group, the Railway Bridge Battalion and the Balloon Battalion (the latter sharing the garrison with the railway units).

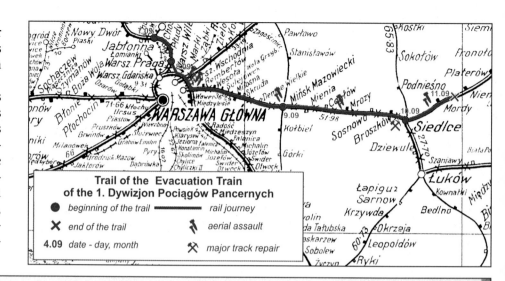

Trail of the Evacuation Train of the 1. Dywizjon Pociągów Pancernych

- ● beginning of the trail
- ✗ end of the trail
- 4.09 date - day, month
- —— rail journey
- ⚔ aerial assault
- ⚒ major track repair

Siedlce station building with visible damage from bombardment and strafing.

The wreckage of the destroyed wagons at Siedlce station.

The 1st Armoured Train Group evacuation train was organized on 7 September. It consisted of about 20 freight wagons supplemented by a two axle armoured artillery wagon (it could be speculated that it was wagon 141164 from the original composition of armoured train "Śmierć"; there was no ammunition available for unknown reason).

Two antiaircraft machine guns were positioned on the tender of the locomotive. The train was filled with surplus supplies, accessories and equipment. A total of about 700 people, including reservist, cadre and officer's families were also accommodated.

On the evening of 7 September, the train left Legionowo. The 20 kilometre stretch to Warszawa – Praga station took 11 hours. Reaching the *Warszawa – Wileńska* station was not possible due to repeated German aircraft attacks. The train returned to Praga station. At dusk, on 8 September the train stared on the route to Rembertów. Along the way the train was again exposed to air attacks. It was late in the night when it reached Rembertów station. The farther travel to Mińsk Mazowiecki, and than past Siedlce (instead of Łuków where the track was completely destroyed), was a journey through torment and anguish. Repeated air attacks, track repair, replen-

ishing engine's water using buckets, and hunger were reoccurring norms of the next three days.

A few kilometres east past the destroyed station of Siedlce, during the night of 11 September the faith of the train was sealed. The further advancement was not possible – the people abandoned the train, many begun searching for any active formations to continue the fight.